PIETY AND POLITICS

PIETY
AND
POLITICS

*American Protestantism
in the World Arena*

ALAN GEYER

JOHN KNOX PRESS • Richmond, Virginia

Library of Congress Catalog Card Number: 63-15198

To the memory of my father
CURTIS BAYLEY GEYER

Preface

Nathaniel Micklem once spoke of "the intermediate country between theology and politics." As both a pastor and a political scientist, I have been living for some time in that "intermediate country"—perhaps "no man's land" better denotes the existential geography. There may be good preachers who, reading these pages, will conclude that they betray the irreverent and irrelevant musings of an "egghead political scientist." On the other hand, there may be, here and there, a stray politician or political scientist who will stumble across this volume and dismiss it as the sort of confusion which only preachers can create when they indulge in worldly matters. I fear there may be justice in both complaints!

There is not only a separation of church and state in the United States: there is a great gulf fixed between churchmanship and citizenship, between religious insight and political wisdom, between theology and political science—all, strangely enough, in a country whose government and politics have been incomparably influenced by Christianity. This book is an attempt to build some conceptual bridges between religion and politics for both churchmen and scholars. It touches upon a wide range of theological studies and social sciences.

My empirical investigation of religious influence upon foreign policy began seven years ago at Boston University in a graduate seminar in diplomacy under Dr. Hubert Gibbs, whose healthy skepticism was a spur to thorough research. That research continued for four years and became a doctoral dissertation with the monstrous title, "American Protestantism and World Politics 1898-1960: A Typological Approach to the Functions of Religion in the Decision-Making Processes of Foreign Policy." This book is a revision of that study. My debt to two other great teachers is beyond calculation. No American scholar has done more than Dean Walter G. Muelder to foster an authentic dialogue between theology and the social sciences. No European scholar has done more than Dr. Nils Ehrenstrom to encourage the academic study of the World Church and of the ethical resources of ecumenical Christianity.

Drs. O. Frederick Nolde and Richard M. Fagley, director and executive secretary of the World Council of Churches' Commission on International Affairs (CCIA), generously set aside substantial time for interviews. The Council on Religion and International Affairs (CRIA) and the Society for Religion in Higher Education both provided critical audiences for an exposition of the central ideas of the book.

My colleagues at Mary Baldwin College, Professors Frank W. Price, Herbert S. Turner, Thomas H. Grafton, and James L. McAllister, Jr., read the original manuscript in whole or in part and made many helpful suggestions. The staff at John Knox Press have been gracious in every way. The personal encouragement and practical assistance of my wife, Joanne, in the difficult work of revision deserve the last and loudest word of appreciation.

Alan Geyer

Contents

INTRODUCTION:
A WORLDLY VIEW OF RELIGION

A Liberian diplomat recently explained the facts of life in African politics to a Baptist audience in Washington. The encounter between Christianity and Communism, he observed, is seriously troubled by a "Christian separatism" which has always baffled Africans. In the Congo, he pointed out, two American missions were established: one by the Northern Baptists and one by the Southern Baptists. He went on: "This, in itself, was perplexing to the Congolese. What heightened their perplexity was the fact that the Northern Baptists operated in the Southern Congo and the Southern Baptists in the Northern Congo." While American Christians are trying to understand tribal conflict among Africans, Africans are trying to understand tribal conflict among American Christians.

Woodrow Wilson was the son of a Presbyterian minister who married the daughter of another Presbyterian minister. Throughout his career, he followed a daily discipline of Bible reading and prayer. "Inheritance and indoctrination made Wilson a Presbyterian; temperament made him an especially devout one—a 'Presbyterian priest' in the words of one Roman Catholic politician who had reason to know."[1]

During the presidential election campaign of 1940, a Philadelphia billboard read:

SAVE YOUR CHURCH

DICTATORS HATE RELIGION

VOTE STRAIGHT REPUBLICAN

Alexis de Tocqueville, that most perceptive observer of all human institutions, observed in the 1830's that it was "the close connection of politics and religion" that was then hastening the decline of Christian influence on the Continent. "The unbelievers of Europe attack the Christians as their political opponents rather than as their religious adversaries; they hate the Christian religion as the opinion of a party much more than as an error of belief; and they reject the clergy less because they are representatives of the church than because they are allies of government."[2]

Jerald C. Brauer has described this generation of Americans as "neo-Puritans" reasserting the ideal that "the saints should rule."

> In America the preachers act like politicians and the politicians talk like preachers. . . . The American public is so concerned, at this particular time in history, to appear as a godly people and nation. . . . It so quickly responds to the religious motif in political life. . . . Americans are convinced that they are a chosen people. Providence has selected them for a special task. Because the American people have been essentially a good people they have become a powerful and rich people.[3]

THE POLITICAL POWER OF RELIGION

Religion and politics intersect at many points on the plane of history, as these five random illustrations demonstrate. This book is an attempt to provide a systematic diagram of the intersections between religion and politics. It is written in the conviction that preachers, laymen, theologians, missionaries, politicians, and social scientists alike do not now possess such a systematic understanding in either thought or action.

At Whitby, Ontario, in July 1947, the International Missionary Council convened to restore the visible bonds of Christian unity which had been shattered during World War II. In a sober assessment of "the world which confronts the Church," the conference report declared: "Although the Church has a life of its own, it touches at every point the life of the world and cannot dissociate itself from it, even if it would."

"Even if it would." These little words suggest the primary assumption of this study: religion is deeply involved in the patterns of political power in American government and in international affairs. This is not a matter of choice: it is a fact of history. It cannot be effaced by the legal hairsplitting to which discussions of separation of church and state so persistently sink. Religion itself is an expression of *power* in personal and social life: it is a dynamic force, not just a static institution circumscribed by law. Those who grasp the fact that religion is a form of power find it difficult to describe that power intelligently. Sermons, annual reports, platform addresses, and resolutions in church bodies alternate violently between trying to prove how powerful an influence religion is and lamenting the fact that religion has so little influence against the hosts of secularism, Communism, crime, and corruption.

Religious leaders are not the only persons who lack perspective and balance in describing religious influence in the world. Social scientists chronically define the religious factor (if they recognize it at all) narrowly and unsystematically, speaking only of such matters as the Catholic vote, moralism, or Hindu-Moslem hostilities. The sentimentality of clergymen in assessing religious influence contrasts sharply with the skepticism of the politician, the anthropologist, and the diplomatic historian.

To these shortcomings of portraying religious power must be added our troubles in understanding political power. The antipolitical bias of Americans in general ("politician" is a word without dignity for "good people") and of religious Americans in particular compounds the trouble. It is difficult enough to grasp the meaning and consequences of political power when the biases of nationalism, partisanship, and self-serving interests are banished—it is impossible to do so from a self-righteous stance which tends to reject politics as immoral, unfortunate, or optional.

A triangle of troubles is completed when one tries to relate either religious or political power to foreign policy. Here one plunges into an ocean of the most tempestuous emotionalism. American attitudes in world affairs have been highly unstable for two generations: a crusade to make the world safe for democracy was followed by a nostalgic isolationism and an ardent pacifism; which were succeeded by a total war to the point of unconditional surrender; which ended with a burst of idealistic internationalism; which gave way to a new crusade against atheistic Communism and a policy of massive retaliation. Just to mention such slogans and moods is to suggest the intense emotional investment Americans have made in their attraction or aversion to various policies in a very short span of their history. Each new policy has cooked up a peculiar stew of religious and political feelings.

A second major assumption of this study is this: American foreign policy is not primarily the product of professional specialists in the State Department. American foreign policy is the way in which the American people decide to confront or ignore the world around them. A free society will not allow its professional policy-makers to become "free agents": policy-makers must be responsive to the psychic currents of public opinion and to the various publics which generate that opinion. The religious and idealistic qualities of American opinion are conspicuous when contrasted with these qualities in other nations. This is not to credit them with a moral superiority: in fact, religious and idealistic impulses have helped to generate the very instability of our foreign policy in the twentieth century.

The churches have already borne a heavier responsibility for American policy than they have been wont to recognize. There is a lack of historic perspective, a default in disciplined understanding and action in the "no-man's land" where the churches actually confront the world in the crucible of concrete events. New crusades are launched, new campaigns waged, new programs promoted to save the present world without understanding why past crusades, campaigns, and programs have been inadequate and, at times, irresponsible. There are patterns in the past which project themselves into the present and the future; responsible leaders will study these patterns and learn from them.

There is much homework to be done by Christians concerned about world affairs in understanding religion itself in its historical and empirical relationships with the world. It is not only important to have a *religious world view:* it is also important to have a *worldly view of religion.* Such a view requires a secular perception of religious influence. Such a view does not pretend to answer the ultimate question as to how any superhuman power may affect politics, foreign policy, or military battles. (Some, if not most, Americans have confidently maintained that our national history has been a unique manifestation of Divine Providence.) Nor does such a view deal directly with what a more Christian foreign policy might be.

Yet even a worldly view of religion must take account of the fact that religion unites its followers with a dimension of life which is beyond purely scientific or secular categories. J. Milton Yinger defines religion in functional terms as a "system of beliefs and practices by means of which a group struggles with the ultimate problems of human life." Among these problems, he lists death, frustration, hostility, and egocentricity—all touching "deep-seated emotional needs, springing from the very nature of man as an individual and as a member of society." [4] Such a definition is peculiarly appropriate to the examination of religion's encounter with world politics. It is the very nature of world politics to thrust these same ultimate problems into bold relief: death, frustration, hostility, self-interest.

As my own research and reflection on the kaleidoscopic relationships between the church and the world have proceeded, one conviction has deepened: it is only in the context of two ultimate concerns that a satisfactory theory of religion and politics may be developed. The first ultimate consists of the universal problems confronted by religious experience; the second is the world-stage itself, this "wide and universal theatre" of international relations. World politics provides the most fateful human

setting for the same ultimate problems with which religion itself
is preoccupied. It is only in the international arena, with its
dramatizing of supreme human triumphs and tragedies in the
lives of nations, that an adequate worldly view of religion may be
established.

But to speak of a theory is to scare off both preachers and
politicians before the end of this first chapter—unless they may
be persuaded that the subject deserves the most serious and
orderly thought. Until quite recently, even political scientists
shared with other Americans a contempt for the very word
"theory" when applied to practical world affairs. Dean Acheson
once complained that "we Americans in our study and writing on
international relations have tended to shun theory and logical
philosophical analysis of historical material." We have been ab-
sorbed in the narratives of our diplomatic history and in the
problems of the League of Nations and the United Nations. The
most urgent need is for "an applicable body of theory." [5]

This book is a plea for *theory* in both religion and politics
and in the intermediate country between them. These introduc-
tory pages, which may prove vexing to some readers, are devoted
to laying the intellectual foundations of the remaining chapters.
Without theory, scholarship becomes trivial and irrelevant. Without sound theory, action becomes random and undisciplined.
Those ardent activists who are impatient for a practical answer
to the world's problems may be disappointed by this insistence
upon a framework of systematic understanding in political ethics.
The particular framework proposed may prove to be less useful
than the encouragement to erect alternatives.

Actually, we do not have a full-blown theory to offer. Our
objective is a more modest one: to sketch a frame of reference
which may clarify some of the fundamental relationships between religion and politics. Surveying the foreign policy of a
single nation in a limited period of its history, we shall identify
patterns of religious influence upon American action between
1898 and 1960, focusing upon Protestantism. The year 1898
marked the self-conscious emergence of the United States as a
great world power. Walter Lippmann, in a landmark essay in

diplomatic history, asserted that "from the promulgation of the Monroe Doctrine to the end of the war with Spain, there was no need for the American people to form a foreign policy. In that long period, the very nature of foreign policy, of what it consists and how it is formed, was forgotten." [6] This long forgetfulness was made possible by a combination of continental isolation and British sea power while the American nation was preoccupied with the expanding frontier, sectional strife, industrialization, and religious revival. At the turn of the century, national energies were released to the international arena.

Religious attention paralleled political interests: there was an increasing international concern in American churches after 1898. The early 1900's witnessed the revitalization of the missionary movement, the development of a social gospel, the unleashing of peace crusades, and the rise of the ecumenical movement —all of which have subsequently shaped relationships between religion and politics. These religious developments occurred during precisely that same period in which the United States was becoming a world power. At the very time that Protestantism was newly seeking to relate itself to all areas of national and international life, foreign policy was moving toward a total diplomacy which, by the late 1940's, would fatefully relate all domestic problems to international problems. Both the religious system and the political system were pushing toward ultimate boundaries of concern.

Within a half-century two ancient loyalties, church and state, were to be recast into distinctly modern forms: "total religion" and "total diplomacy." Two competing "loyalty-systems" compelled the re-thinking of all of the political doctrines and strategies of Protestantism. Through global conversations afforded by the ecumenical movement, Americans learned that Germans and Norwegians and Indians and Japanese were also trying to think through the meaning of this century's totalitarian struggle between the claims of God and the claims of Caesar. The theme of conflicting loyalties is fundamental to our worldly view of religion.

Conflict is an enduring characteristic of human life, and that, not simply between the church and the world, but among worldly centers of loyalty as well. Church-state doctrines and sociological theories of religion have ignored this dimension of conflict among states in describing religious action in the world. The trouble with most church-state doctrines is that they are purely domesticated in trying to locate Christianity somewhere within the state. Whether or not the legal doctrine of national sovereignty is made explicit, there is an assumption that the nation-state defines the outer boundaries of Christian concern and influence. This is both ethically cramped and historically short-sighted. The state is not the largest arena within which the church exists: the church has a trans-national life which touches a vast plurality of states. This whole realm of ethical and legal discussion would be better identified as "church-and-states."

Sociologists of religion, beginning with Max Weber, have also domesticated religion within a single unit which they call society or the social order. They have pictured, brilliantly at times, the tension between the church and the world—but they have been preoccupied with the way in which the church has been influenced by such domestic forces as industrialization and the class struggle. Troeltsch, H. Richard Niebuhr, Yinger, and others have taken over Weber's "church-sect" typology to contrast the opposite tendencies of Christianity to accommodate to society and to withdraw from society. Society, however, is not simply one political entity: it is fragmented into societies which come into conflict with each other. Christianity cannot be contained within any single society.

What is true of the legalistic approach to church-and-state, as well as the sociological study of religion, has been generally true of the social sciences in their most secular aspects. They have had a built-in nationalist bias which has prevented them from comprehending international forces and events. This is not, however, a bias of patriotic passion: it is the distortion which results from theoretical models which are too puny to fit the facts of variety, conflict, and change within the whole world to which the church, the state, and all other human institutions must adjust. Social science theory—in political science, economics, and sociology alike—has had a fixation on the internal phenomena of societies and nation-states.[7] There has been a chronic failure to achieve a theoretical breakthrough to the universal theater where the history of our times is being made.

Nevertheless, theological studies and the social sciences together have amassed a vast quantity of information and speculation about the influence of religious power in the political arena. The theory of religion and politics which this study unfolds seeks to give order and meaning to these data in a comprehensive way. The fruits of previous study may be grouped according to an inventory of the various functions which religion performs in world politics. Thus, religion may be described as a system of international communications, as a source of international law, as a public opinion audience for a professional elite, as a determinant of voting behavior, as a source of hostility to policy-makers, as a sustainer of military morale, and so on. (For the full inventory of sixty such functions, see Appendix II.)

Such a secular inventory may help to focus further studies in this field. It may also serve as a practical catalogue helping church leaders to achieve a more self-conscious awareness of the richness and variety of religious influence in the world. While it is hardly a handbook for Christian statesmanship, it lists some of the parallel problems which religious leadership shares with political leadership (in addition to handshaking, tongue-wagging, and baby-kissing). There are, for example, nearly a hundred methods of implementing official foreign policy in any given country; Department of State policy-makers are obliged to select the most appropriate and efficient mix of these methods for a particular policy to be responsible and effective. Religious leaders are similarly obliged to take stock of the appropriateness and the mix of methods which are uniquely at their disposal. This is not simply a matter of yielding to secular conceptions of strategy: it is faithful stewardship of available religious resources. If the churches have their own peculiar points of access in the process of shaping and implementing American policy, church leaders have an obligation to perceive those points of access objectively, with all of their possibilities for good or for evil.

The full inventory readily reveals two opposite features of religion commonly recognized by historians and social scientists: its cohesiveness and its divisiveness. Everywhere and always, religion both unites and separates. Religious behavior generates both loyalty and conflict among persons and groups. These two basic categories of loyalty and conflict provide a dialectical foundation—a dramatic tension—for a worldly view of religion. "Think over the great dramas of all times," Robert MacIver once proposed, "and you will find that they concentrate on the issue of clashing loyalties."[8] From *Antigone* to *Hamlet,* this concentration is apparent; both of these tragedies concern conflicts between personal and political loyalties. The political arena dramatizes the themes inherent in a truly prophetic ethic, for it is in that arena that conflicting loyalties are most vividly portrayed.

There is thus a duality of religious influence in the world. Religion may exert a power of identification with politics ("God bless America!") and a power of transcendence above politics ("In Christ there is no East or West"). Another aspect of this dual role is suggested by the distinction between the words "sanction" and "sanctuary." Webster defines "sanction" as an "influence which impels to moral action." Its Latin root is the verb *sanctio:* to render sacred or inviolable. Religion is peculiarly equipped to make political actions seem sacred or inviolable ("One nation, under God, indivisible"). A "sanctuary," on the other hand, is "a sacred and inviolable asylum; a place of refuge; immunity from law by entering such a place." The Christian religion is not only a ministry to the state; it is a ministry to the soul ("Rock of Ages, cleft for me, Let me hide myself in Thee"). Faith is thus a mixture of public and private affairs. Again, Christianity acts in both a prophetic role and a pastoral role—it possesses a power of upsetting the world and a capacity for reconciling its people, a militant mission and a mediatory office.

Religion is not a simple duality. It becomes involved in a pattern of triangular relationships in world politics: a triangle formed by the church, the state, and the world. To diagram these relationships in a systematic way, a six-fold scheme seems arithmetically appropriate:

1. Religion as a source of loyalty
2. Religion as a sanction for political loyalty
3. Religion as a sanction for political conflict
4. Religion as a source of political conflict
5. Religion as a sanctuary from political conflict
6. Religion as a reconciler of political conflict

These are proposed quite simply as the six basic functions of religion in world politics. They comprise a "typology," or a set of "types" or categories around which we can organize our understanding of the variety of religious influences in the political arena. They provide the architecture of the theory which is set forth in succeeding chapters. (See chart, Appendix I.)

A creative tension must be maintained among all six of these functions if Christianity is to remain true to its own genius in the world. The six types not only describe the range of Christian action in the world; they prescribe that action as well. But it may be said of them, as Troeltsch spoke of the interaction of the church, sect, and mystic tendencies within Protestantism, that they

> will meet the fate which always awaits every fresh creation of religious and ethical thought: they will render indispensable services and they will develop profound energies, but they will never fully realize their actual ideal intention within the sphere of our earthly struggle and conflict. . . . This is the cause of that ceaseless tension which drives man onward yet gives him the sense that he can never realize his ethical ideal.[9]

A POSITIVE THEORY OF CONFLICT

It is not only religious loyalty which generates tensions; political loyalty generates its own tensions among parties and nations. Foreign policy is formulated and implemented with reference to the persisting fact of conflict among national loyalties. Herbert Butterfield describes this quality:

> It is characteristic of diplomacy . . . that it functions in cases where wills are in conflict and power is involved—cases where,

if there were no such method of negotiation, the parties concerned would be making a direct appeal to force. And even
where the struggle is a purely diplomatic one, the force of the
respective states is not annulled, but is rather transmuted and
transformed.[10]

All "realists" emphasize the fact of conflict in international relations—the "struggle for power" is their favorite version of conflict
as a law of political life. There must, however, be a theory which
helps us to understand the nature of conflict in terms of its
dynamic and moral qualities.

Since 1957, a journal called *Conflict Resolution* has provided
a distinctive approach to international theory which has much
to contribute to our ethical appreciation of world politics. The
terms "conflict" and "resolution" indicate the concern to combine realism with imaginative action; they also imply that international conflict is not simply to be judged as bad but that it
may be managed for good ends in human affairs. Those whose
moral inhibitions lead them to seek to eliminate all conflict by
"good will" or "understanding" misunderstand both ethics and
politics.

This is not really a new view of political realities. Our own
American political institutions possess a unique genius in guar-
anteeing a pattern of tensions without which personal freedom
and social progress could not have been achieved. A two-party
system, the separation of powers, an economy of competitive
enterprise, a court system based on the adversary principle, a
federal system which makes the national government and the
states eternal competitors for a share of sovereignty—the fundamentals of our government involve the deliberate staging of
conflicts in the belief that precious human values depend upon
those very conflicts. A senior political scientist, E. E. Schattschneider, has recently written a lucid essay in which he describes
democratic government as "the greatest single instrument for the
socialization of conflict in the American community. . . . Government thrives on conflict. . . . The grand strategy of politics
deals with public policy concerning conflict."[11]

Both ethics and politics require, therefore, an appreciation of the positive functions of conflict, which include: (1) the challenge to maximum personal and group effort; (2) the strengthening of meaningful loyalties to groups as small as a high school and as large as a nation; (3) the clarification of group purposes and goals; (4) the channeling of personal tensions into satisfying group efforts; (5) the prevention of a monopoly of power which imposes uniformity and stifles creativity; (6) the voluntary settlement of disputes; and (7) the encouragement of social change. That conflict is also dangerous and destructive, supremely so in a generation threatened with annihilation by weapons of its own making, simply sharpens our awareness of the razor's edge between freedom and responsibility. To resolve conflict, therefore, is not to abolish it: it is to institutionalize conflict. And to institutionalize conflict is to subordinate it to common values and to processes of co-operation, to make it productive of human good, and to reduce its destructiveness.

In more colorful language, the possibilities and the limitations of such a positive view of conflict have been suggested by Frederick L. Schuman, a political scientist sensitive to the moral efforts of men and nations:

> If the Temple of Man can slowly be reared on foundations of swords beaten into plowshares, the result will not be Paradise, even if the structure is finally completed. Men will not thereby become saints nor be magically liberated from unreason. They will struggle with themselves and with one another for goals ignoble and noble, and find many of their conflicts difficult of resolution. But the result, we may reasonably believe, will be an escape from an Inferno wherein men like devils torture one another to death in a vain quest for salvation. And without such escape, none can sensibly hope for betterment of our common lot or for a chance for human self-realization.[12]

DECISION-MAKING AND FOREIGN POLICY

Both ethics and politics also have to do with the making of decisions. Christians concerned about the ethical dimensions of world politics have much to learn from the analysis of decision-making which has developed in foreign policy studies in the past decade.[13] If conflict is a category which identifies the arena of world politics, decision-making is the category which focuses upon the role of the human actors in that arena: statesmen and the publics which influence them. Decision-making is a process which brings clarity to the study of international relations—a field as noteworthy for its chaotic thought as for its chaotic action.

Decision-making is, moreover, a concept which unavoidably makes basic ethical assumptions. To decide is to exercise freedom, creativity, power, responsibility. It is to have some ability to reason in the face of meaningful alternatives. As one carefully analyzes the process of making policy decisions in government, it becomes readily apparent that ethical and technical matters mingle with each other at every major step. Rationally, eight such steps are involved in the making of foreign policy:

1. **Valuation:** the choice of policy goals, customarily related to some conception of the national interest
2. **Intelligence:** the perception and analysis of a problem tending to threaten the national interest
3. **Recommendation:** proposal(s) for a decision
4. **Prescription:** the decision to act
5. **Promulgation:** publication of the decision (the public to whom the decision is announced may be restricted for reasons of national security)
6. **Approval:** response of co-ordinate decision-makers and the public
7. **Application:** enforcement of the decision
8. **Appraisal:** measurement of the adequacy of policy in achieving the chosen goals

This orderly model can be misleading, however, when the actual processes of foreign policy are examined. Decision-making is not necessarily the logical procedure which such a model suggests. Policy often becomes the sum of vaguely related actions, expressing an uneasy, inconsistent compromise. Frequently, policy is formulated, but fails of implementation because it is blocked or changed somewhere down the line. Franklin D. Roosevelt, famed as he was for expanding the powers of the modern Presidency, once complained of bureaucratic obstacles to Marriner Eccles:

The Treasury is so large and far-flung in its practices that I find it almost impossible to get the action and results I want —even with Henry [Morgenthau] there. But the Treasury is not to be compared with the State Department. You should go through the experience of trying to get any changes in the thinking, policy and action of the career diplomats and then you'd know what a real problem was. But the Treasury and the State Department put together are nothing compared with the Na-a-vy. The Admirals are really something to cope with— I should know. To change anything in the Na-a-vy is like punching a feather bed. You punch it with your right and you punch it with your left until you are finally exhausted, and then you find the damn bed just as it was before you started punching.[14]

Another aspect of the way in which foreign policy actually is made is the sheer complexity of the machinery of policy. Case studies of particular policy decisions have trouble locating the persons most responsible for those decisions: whether they are high or low in the hierarchy, or whether the initiative has come from persons in Congress or in the Executive branch. Few policymakers see themselves as powerful enough to be held accountable for policy.[15] As the sense of personal responsibility is weakened, spiritual and ethical sanctions tend to weaken also.

The complexity and impersonality of the "foreign policy machine" are not difficult to demonstrate. The Constitution itself, with its separation of powers and system of checks and balances, provided for a combination of executive and legislative decision-making: Presidential appointments and treaties, and Congressional action on appropriations, the maintenance of armed forces, the declaration of war, and the regulation of international commerce. The Senate was assigned a special role in the ratification of treaties and in advice and consent concerning appointments.

Both executive and legislative machinery have become increasingly elaborate. The Department of State, with its policy planning staff, bureaus, offices, desks, diplomatic hierarchy and consular services, is perhaps the most obvious agency of policy subordinate to the President. But total diplomacy, especially since 1947, has created a long list of other executive agencies, including: the National Security Council, the Department of Defense, the Joint Chiefs of Staff, the Central Intelligence Agency, the United States Information Agency, the Agency for International Development, the Arms Control and Disarmament Agency, the Bureau of the Budget, and such cabinet-level departments as Treasury, Commerce, Labor, and Agriculture which maintain major staffs for international responsibilities in their fields.

Similarly, the co-ordinate role of Congress in foreign policy is not confined to its most obvious committees, the Senate Foreign Relations Committee and the House Foreign Affairs Committee. The Finance and Ways and Means committees processed the crucial Trade Expansion Act in 1962. Appropriations committees annually determine the fate of foreign aid programs and the adequacy of diplomatic facilities. Committees on Armed Services, Agriculture, Commerce, Labor, and Merchant Marine and Fisheries concern themselves with the international activities of all the executive agencies in their fields. The Judiciary and Un-American Activities committees are preoccupied with immigration and subversion, Government Operations with the entire policy apparatus, Banking and Currency with international finance, Interior and Insular Affairs with Pacific trust territories, and Public Works with the St. Lawrence Seaway. The Joint Committee on Atomic Energy, paralleling the independent Atomic Energy Commission, influences policy decisions in such internationally sensitive realms as nuclear testing and arms control. The Joint Committee on the Economic Report takes stock of American commitments abroad in the context of domestic resources and growth.[16]

Responsibility for American foreign policy is therefore extremely diffused. This diffusion troubles the press and the politician, alarms the moralist, and alienates the public—all of whom demand to know "who's responsible?!" The investigation of policy decisions is a very slippery enterprise. In an age of total diplomacy, it is somewhat artificial to study any policy in isolation from other policy areas. All of the basic organs of government share decision-making duties affecting international relations. Every area of basic national policy, including domestic policy, has become a problem for foreign policy. There is a cumulative factor in world politics which tends to discourage both the earnest researcher and the eager citizen: foreign policy "merges with a swelling stream of other human happenings; and we cannot trace its effects with any exactness once it has entered the fluid substance of history." [17] Confusion is added to diffusion when allowance is made for the practices of secrecy and propaganda employed by a security-sensitive government.

What impact does religion actually bring to bear upon these vast bureaucracies of decision-making? The answer to that question must be sought in the ethical and spiritual qualities of the decision-makers and those who seek to influence them. Both the ends and means of foreign policy involve value judgments as to the meaning of "the national interest." Just what the national interest is at any particular time may be a matter of ethical and political controversy: it is not nearly as self-evident as Hans Morgenthau and other "realists" would have us believe.[18]

The public helps to shape any current definition of the national interest through its own widely shared ideal of a national mission. That ideal may be vague and inarticulate; it may rest upon a distorted perception of world politics. Nevertheless, the ideal of national mission has an objective reality in the sense that it imposes mass restraints upon policy-makers. Religious influence upon this ideal is a recurring motif of this study. Religion is endowed with a peculiar power for channeling public energies: its idealistic and emotional properties help to set the limits of basic national policies. Public opinion, when aroused on matters of principle, may seize upon a particular personality or policy or territory and sanctify it as absolutely vital to the national interest. The statesman may dissent from this judgment: he may be persuaded that circumstances have altered national interests, that a more pragmatic and flexible attitude is required, that the occasion is ripe for bargain and compromise—but the public judgment of principle tends to prevail.[19]

The capacity of religion to sanctify or reject public policy tends to be exercised through its leaders—decision-influencers if not decision-makers. Gabriel Almond's pioneering study of public opinion and foreign policy asserted that clergymen and influential laymen possess a power as "opinion elites" which they do not understand with sufficient clarity.[20] The instability of mass moods underlying foreign policy provides religious influence with special access to any current expression of the national mission. Religious leaders can trigger the most opposite and contradictory responses in public opinion. This study moves toward a theory of religious leadership which can appreciate the need to discipline the moral energies which the churches impart to the body politic. The six-fold typology will be developed as a pattern for such a discipline. Will Durant once declared that "co-ordinated energy is the last word in ethics and politics, and perhaps in logic and metaphysics, too." [21]

That religious leaders are more often decision-influencers than decision-makers does not exempt them from an obligation to understand the internal structure of decision-making of the United States government. The human burdens and dilemmas, ethical and spiritual as well as technical, borne by decision-makers deserve something like pastoral empathy. Elder's description of the policy machine takes account of these inner, personal realities of decision-making in American foreign policy:

> In a sense, the policy machine is nothing more than man writ large, with both his limitations and his potentialities, carrying within itself the frustrations, the interests, and the emotions of contemporary society. For man and the men who make policies are not machines, nor would we have them become mere automatons. Indeed, the ultimate goal of American foreign policy is to preserve and develop the opportunities of mankind to remain human, yet to encourage man to find in himself new humanity.[22]

The decisions made by the United States government in this age of mutual terror will be made by human beings, more or less responsive to the moral qualities of the American public. Even before the appearance of nuclear weapons, the same generation was being taught by the churches to see that religion has to do with all of life and by schools and statesmen to see that politics has to do with all of life. Compartmentalization between religion and politics in this kind of world is the most serious kind of schizophrenia. Virtually every aspect of personal and social living has become a political question in the twentieth century. Now the decisions are being made which will determine whether man himself will continue his life as lord of the Creation. These are inescapably political decisions; they are profoundly religious decisions as well.

RELIGION
AS A SOURCE OF LOYALTY

THE IDEAL OF LOYALTY

The first function of religion in world politics is to unite its believers with a supreme center of loyalties. All other loyalties derive their meaning from this supreme center. Obedience and faithfulness to God are absolute requirements in Hebrew and Christian scriptures. The commandments announce these requirements: "You shall have no other gods before me . . . for I the LORD your God am a jealous God." [1] The Revised Standard Version gave a heightened emphasis to this theme by translating the Hebrew *chesed* as "loyalty" or "steadfast love" instead of "mercy," which had been the most common rendering in the King James Version. Thus, the Psalms "sing of loyalty and of justice," [2] and the Proverbs proclaim that "loyalty and faithfulness preserve the king." [3] These religio-political expressions of the word for "loyalty" proceed from the distinctive qualities of Old Testament religion. Snaith suggests that the full meaning of *chesed* is "covenant-love," thus relating it to the central doctrine of both covenants or testaments. This love is expressed in mutual obligation between God and the people of God. "The original use of the Hebrew *chesed* is to denote that attitude of loyalty and faithfulness which both parties to a covenant should observe towards each other." [4]

Christian obedience in the New Testament combines both ultimate ("We must obey God rather than men")[5] and institutional ("Obey your leaders and submit to them")[6] qualities.

The religious fellowship is committed to divine commandments which control both its internal life and its relationship to the world. Paul Lehmann finds the foundation and pattern of Christian behavior in the *koinonia*, the beloved community of the New Covenant, which manifests the operation of divine providence in human history:

> The *koinonia* is the outpost of God's judgment upon every pattern and structure which seeks to preserve and to justify itself by the idolatry of the status quo. And the *koinonia* is the outpost of God's renewal, establishing new patterns and structures, commensurate with God's new possibilities of living on the other side of those which are played out. The ethical reality of the Christian life is being, in fact and in anticipation, ready for God's next move.[7]

It is the very nature of the religious fellowship, thus conceived, to regard all other associations in a relative and provisional way.

Protestant, Catholic, and Jewish communities in the United States have all been marked by a growing self-assertion in the face of what they have regarded as the relativism of a secular age. Salo Baron, in his discussion of the relationship between nationalism and religion, has observed that "even liberal Protestantism and Reform Judaism have tended in recent years to search for more absolute values and demand more rigid observance. . . . There has been a universal quest for religious absolutes to satisfy the cravings for spiritual security of a generation which had come to cherish security almost above everything else." [8] Modern nationalism, with quasi-religious qualities of its own, is thus confronted with a new absolutism of faith.

The political expression of religious absolutism is not necessarily a rigid, uncompromising legalism. Butterfield declares that the loyal Christian is provided with the most relevant ethical equipment:

> Precisely because he can hold fast to spiritual truths—not turning any mundane programme or temporal ideal into the absolute of absolutes—the Christian has it in his power to be more flexible in respect of all subordinate matters, and to ally himself with whatever may be the best for the world at a given moment. . . . The Christian is particularly called to

carry his thinking outside that framework which a nation or a political party or a social system or an accepted regime or a mundane theology provides. Even the preservation of what we may love as the existing order of things—even Anglo-Saxon ideals and western values—are not the absolute values for the Christian.[9]

Political ethics for the faithful Christian is not, as both his friends and his critics have caricatured it, an unyielding moralism which must somehow be made to bend to the realities of this world. It proceeds, rather, from a radically corporate experience nourished and sustained in the vitality of an historic community. This community has an organic relationship with the world. It is corporate in two fundamental senses. Vertically, it is the continuing embodiment by the Christian fellowship of that Ultimate Being whose life was made visible in the Incarnation—it is the Body of Christ. Horizontally, it is this fellowship's living expression of its absolute loyalty in practicing its Covenant-obligations among its own members and with the world.

The "Opinion Gap"

While Christian values are ideally expected to control the political behavior of Christian people, those values cannot be immediately translated into political behavior. There must be authoritative pronouncements by church leaders which interpret the meaning of faith in policy matters and which are commended to their constituents. Leaders tend to measure the loyalty of their constituents in terms of agreement with their pronouncements. In a free society, church leaders have only limited powers with which to enforce loyalty to official views: they must depend primarily upon education and moral persuasion. There is apparently an inevitable gap between pronouncements on policy issues and the opinions which actually prevail among the constituents. In practical terms, this gap may be considered as a measure of the lack of loyalty to church leaders, although rank-and-file opinions may actually express a more authentic Christian viewpoint on particular issues.

Politicians often perceive this "opinion gap" in the churches.

Such a failure of Christians to achieve consensus may subject the politician to conflicting pressures from religion, but those very differences tend to weaken the influence of Christianity and to allow the politician to be more responsive to secular than to religious pressures. Factors determining the size of the "opinion gap" in the churches include: (1) latent or unintended influences of the leaders themselves which undermine their intentional influence; (2) disagreements among leaders; (3) rigidities of religious organization; and (4) the pull of secular loyalties on church members. Similar factors operate in all groups which seek to influence national policy: leaders can only "deliver" a fraction of their constituents.

(1) Latent Influences of Leadership

In an analysis of public moods which have alternated between isolationism and internationalism, Fensterwald distinguishes between the intent and the effect of religious influence upon American opinion. While most American churches appear from their pronouncements to be "staunchly and outspokenly 'internationalist,'" their own "policies, principles, and teachings may well influence their members in the adoption of ultra-nationalistic attitudes."[10] Fensterwald does not elaborate the contention, but the force of it will be demonstrated in succeeding chapters in this study. One illustration may suffice at this point: the investment of religious funds in corporations holding generous defense contracts from the United States government may tend to offset the influence of peace-minded leaders in the churches who are pressing for disarmament and for an economy which is not so much at the mercy of government spending. The latent functions of religion in influencing public policy may operate at cross-purposes with the manifest functions, even superseding the latter in some instances.

(2) Fragmentation of Leadership

Pronouncements on controversial national issues frequently find religious leaders as divided among themselves as the general public. It is difficult to win support for pronouncements which do not reflect a genuine consensus of representative leaders. There are enduring controversies of a theological and ethical nature, such as pacifism versus non-pacifism, which prevent religious sanctions from gaining uniform support.

The patterns of authority which bind religious leaders together may significantly affect their influence upon public policy. Central control is maximized within or among denominations to the extent to which binding commitments govern the degree of co-ordination; it is minimized to the extent to which individuals meet as representatives or ambassadors from a constituency to which they feel responsible.[11] It seems quite likely that those Protestant leaders most exercised about international affairs are somewhat marginal to the constituencies which they are supposed to represent. Other leaders—perhaps a majority on most foreign policy issues—may respond with indifference or opposition to the churches' own official spokesmen on those issues. A denominational board of peace may not enjoy the confidence of those denominational decision-makers who actually have much more prestige and influence than the world-minded brethren on the board of peace. Without the confidence and support of power figures, the churches' witness is a weak one.

(3) Hardening of the Ecclesiastical Arteries

Religious leaders confront within their all-too-human ecclesiastical institutions the same obstacles of bureaucratic block and change which policy-makers confront within the government. Bilheimer illuminates these problems in the field of ecumenical action by complaining that "the official representatives of the churches in the ecumenical movement may be so tempted to interpret ecumenical insight and judgment in terms congenial to their own constituencies as to rob those insights and judgments of their power."[12] Ecumenical action is described as a two-way process combining a movement upward and a movement downward. The movement upward is the formation of a common mind from denominations through national councils to world conferences and the preparation for those conferences. It is Bilheimer's judgment that the ecumenical movement has been more successful in forming a common mind than in "throwing its agreements and concerns back upon its constituency." [13] In the movement downward, where no coercion but only moral persuasion is possible, policies confront such institutional rigidities as: (a) the natural inflexibility of institutions which are sanctioned by religious doctrines; (b) vested interests in property, program, work, and viewpoint; (c) the self-generation of pride; and (d) the tendency of all institutions to be self-perpetuating regardless of their effectiveness.[14]

The movement downward in religious organization, denominational or ecumenical, is seldom if ever one of unobstructed progress from top leaders to average laymen. In foreign policy matters, religious pronouncements commonly do not filter down to the local constituencies at all.

(4) Trivialization of Church Membership

In modern, multigroup American society, most church members also belong to a number of other constituencies in which secular values are dominant. The intensity of these alternative loyalties may tend to diminish the intensity of religious loyalties. Religious affiliation for many persons becomes more nominal and less decisive: it is religion at a low temperature. Such a trivialization of religious allegiance results in the extreme attenuation of commitment to specifically religious values.[15] Religious pronouncements on foreign policy matters may be less influential for most church members than the viewpoints of a chamber of commerce, a Rotary Club, a labor union, a bar association, the American Legion, or the League of Women Voters. In fact, among both religious and secular elites there is powerful opposition to genuine controversy between religious and secular viewpoints. Many church members never become exposed to the distinctive insights of their own Christian tradition as they relate to world affairs—either because of institutional rigidities within the church or secular pressures from without. Even when religion attains a high temperature of emotional intensity, its only function in public affairs may be to bless whatever self-interest ordains. In such persons, church membership has indeed become trivialized as an absolute loyalty controlling other loyalties.

MEASURING THE "OPINION GAP"

Several studies of the "opinion gap" between pronouncements and popular attitudes in the churches have helped to provide a graphic appreciation of the seriousness of the problem. Glock and Ringer, in a survey of the attitudes of Episcopalian ministers and parishioners on political issues, assembled data on the degree of support of denominational positions on international issues. Their investigation took place in 1951-1952 and compared clergy and lay attitudes with the official pronouncements adopted by the Protestant Episcopal Church in its triennial meetings, at which all American dioceses and overseas missions are represented. Glock and Ringer found that parishioners were in essential agreement with the stand officially taken by their denomination on only one issue: support for the United Nations. This was interpreted partly in terms of the traditional ties between the Episcopal Church and Great Britain and the fact that internationalism in the twentieth century has been based upon a close American-British alliance.

A wide divergency of lay attitudes did not prevent bold pronouncements on some other issues—especially when such statements did not trespass upon economic interests, where pronouncements tended to be mild and equivocal. Paradoxically, however, the very lack of consensus which weakened collective opposition to bold pronouncements also weakened the authority of the denominational leaders who framed them.

Within denominational organization, the parish minister was identified as the crucial link in communicating church policy to the church's membership and as the individual most subject to cross pressures where conflict arises between church policy on an issue and how his parishioners feel on this issue. Ministers tend to identify with church policy despite the opposition of many parishioners. The same desire to keep from alienating parishioners which leads to mild and equivocal pronouncements on many political issues may, however, dissuade the minister from communicating bolder pronouncements to his own local constituency.[16]

The "opinion gap" is not solely a Protestant problem. Protestants are prone to exaggerate the ability of Roman Catholics to present a solid front on political issues. In an opinion survey of "the Catholic mind" of a Southern parish, Fichter found that even "ideal types" (those who had shown the "most Catholic behavior" in fulfilling church obligations) dissented significantly from official teachings on political matters. Only 38 per cent supported the Church's position that atomic bombs should not be dropped on civilians in a future war (presumably, Russian civilians); just 26 per cent accepted the principle of desegregation in the schools. On all issues, domestic and foreign, the average of support by "ideal Catholics" was 57 per cent.[17] While Catholic leadership may be relatively unified and more tightly organized than Protestant leadership, it is evident that religious elites in all groups fail to command solid support on many foreign policy questions.

Reinhold Niebuhr, after praising the quality of papal teachings in political matters, remarked with twinkled eye to a panel at the 1960 annual meeting of the American Political Science Association: "The real issue in the 1960 campaign is not 'How much Vatican control of American government will result if Senator Kennedy is elected?' but 'How can we help the Vatican to have more influence over the American hierarchy's political attitudes?' " Niebuhr was suggesting that even Catholic leadership is much less monolithic than is supposed by many Protestants, when it comes to issues of public controversy.

The ideological struggle with world Communism has introduced new elements into mass attitudes on foreign policy. In a celebrated study of the American mind as it focused on the problems of Communism and threats to civil liberties in the summer of 1954, Stouffer reported that there was little statistical evidence for a national anxiety neurosis over these issues at the level of local leadership. However, among those most worried about Communist infiltration, the antireligious aspects of Communist beliefs were most frequently mentioned. Moreover, church-attenders were found to be less tolerant in the maintenance of constitutional liberties than were non-church-attenders.[18] This local picture contrasts with conspicuous efforts of national leaders in the denominations and in the ecumenical movement at that time to protect civil liberties and to prevent anti-Communist hysteria. Perhaps most conspicuous was the 1953 appearance of Methodist Bishop G. Bromley Oxnam, a president of the World Council of Churches, before the House Un-American Activities Committee and his subsequent criticisms of the investigating practices of the committee.[19] It may well be, therefore, that sermons preached against the evils of atheistic Communism in local churches in 1953 and 1954 tended to offset the national pronouncements and actions concerning Communism, the dangers of conformity, and the threats to civil liberties.

In practice, it is thus apparent, the ideal of Christian loyalty does not mean uniform support for the official positions of the churches in matters of national policy. It is both an asset and a liability of Christian strategy in political life that many of the world's conflicts are embraced within the human fellowship of the church itself.

RELIGION
AS A SANCTION FOR LOYALTY

The second function of religion in world politics is to interpret political loyalty as a religious obligation. The Psalmist sang: "Blessed is the nation whose God is the Lord, the people whom he has chosen as his heritage!"[1] The prophets continually called the Hebrew people back to their mission as a chosen people. Jesus instructed the Pharisees: "Render therefore to Caesar the things that are Caesar's, and to God the things that are God's."[2] Paul wrote to the church at Rome: "Let every person be subject to the governing authorities. For there is no authority except from God, and those that exist have been instituted by God."[3] In various ways do the Scriptures sanction political loyalty as a religious duty.

RELIGION AND THE AMERICAN CHARACTER

Notwithstanding the separation of church and state in the United States, no modern nation has had a greater tendency to interpret political loyalty as a religious duty. In 1889, on the eve of the decade in which the United States was to emerge as a world power, Lord Bryce published his *American Commonwealth* as an Englishman's picture of the political life of the land. His description was not narrowly political: the very title suggests his background concern for intellectual and social phenomena and the role which he assigned to the Puritan ideal of commonwealth in creating the institutions of American government. Bryce noted these distinctive characteristics of life in the United States: (a) Christianity is, in fact if not in name, the national religion; (b) the world view of average Americans is shaped by the Bible and Christian theology; (c) Americans attribute progress and prosperity to Divine favor; (d) political thought is deeply influenced by such Puritan emphases as the doctrine of original sin; (e) American constitutional government is peculiarly legalistic; (f) American religion is marked by emotional fervor; and (g) the social activities of American religion are singularly developed.[4]

In describing the influence upon political institutions of a religion which was supremely confident yet preoccupied with evil, legalistic, activistic, and emotional, Bryce provided more than seventy years ago a striking anticipation of recent discussion of the American character as it affects politics and foreign policy. Earlier in the same decade, the German historian, Leopold von Ranke, more generally testified to the interpenetration of political and religious energies in modern nationalism: "In most periods of world history nations were held together by religious ties alone."[5] There has been an historic interplay between nationalism and religion: "Positively or negatively, religions served as the most powerful vehicle of both nationalization and denationalization, while receiving in turn enormous stimuli from the patriotic, ethnic and cultural loyalties of their adherents." These nationality-forming and nationality-preserving features of religion have been well understood and successfully used by the political leaders of nations and empires.[6]

This interpenetration of religious and political loyalties is of fundamental importance in understanding American foreign policy. Two writers not at all disposed to view religious influence sentimentally have declared that "nothing fixes the quality of a nation's foreign policy more than the character of the body politic from whence it springs." How a people "look upon religion, ethics, the individual person, and the state must assert itself in the entire political life of the nation, whether domestic or foreign; it sets the goals of policy and marks out the avenues of approach to them."[7]

In the American body politic, the religious component has been especially vital and fruitful. In no other Western nation has religious influence upon government and public policy been more pervasive or profound. This is not to say that organized religion directly or effectively intervenes in all the processes of policy-making. Rather, religious influence is largely an expression of continuities of national character, most deposited long before the United States became a world power. Both political and religious leaders are obliged to take stock of these historical realities. Brogan echoes Bryce: "The connection between morals, the law, and politics is old and not exclusively American. But, in America, the connection has been made closer by the religious inheritance of the American people, and by the American belief in the necessity and desirability of legislation to put down manifest evils."[8]

This distinctive mixture of political and religious sentiments, of public and private spirituality, of legal and moral doctrines, of national and Christian faiths has been termed "the Puritan ethos." Puritan Protestantism molded a collective unity of religious and ethical attitudes which has affected all later generations of Americans, even Catholics and Jews from southern and eastern Europe. It was in America, the one major Western nation for whom the social contract of seventeenth- and eighteenth-century philosophers did not remain simply a myth of obscure origins, that the purposeful and recorded acts of nationalization took place: mass migration, Declaration of Independence, Constitution. It was in America that this historic contract was to seem most like a covenant between a chosen people and its Sovereign Lord. While every nation has some version of Messianism in its national character, America seemed to have special warrant to regard itself as "the darling of divine providence."[9] Not only the early Puritans but Jeffersonian rationalists and romantic poets attributed American fortunes to the hand of God: here was born a "new Israel," a new "Promised Land." The ancient community of the Covenant had become the American Commonwealth. Religious loyalty and political loyalty were reunited as in the Israel of Old Testament times.

Calvinism, most conspicuously in New England, linked the doctrine of the Covenant with American constitutionalism and politics. While the intentional influence of Puritan leaders was authoritarian, it contributed inadvertently to the democratic, libertarian, and humanitarian impulses of the new nation. "That magistrates were limited by compact, that government should be by laws and not by men, that the covenant was not annulled by any serious violation of the terms—these principles were declared no less emphatically in Puritan theory than in the Declaration of Independence."[10] The limiting of power—separation into three branches, a bicameral Congress, a federal system of states —is perhaps the most characteristic feature of American constitutional government. John Locke, the philosopher of Puritan England, insisted upon the restraint of power, within and outside of government—to secure the natural rights of "life, liberty, and property." But two generations earlier, John Cotton, the Puritan theologian who came from Old to New England, warned against

> the danger of allowing to any mortal man an inordinate measure of power to speak great things. . . . Whatever power he hath received, he hath a corrupt nature that will improve it in one thing or other. . . . It is therefore most wholesome for magistrates and officers in church and commonwealth never to affect more liberty and authority than will do them good: for whatever transcendent power is given will certainly overrun those that give it and those that receive it. . . . It is necessary therefore that all power that is on earth be limited, church-power or other.[11]

Whatever may be the affinities between twentieth-century Americans and their ancestors in colonial religion and constitutional convention, it is important to recognize that the basic structures of American government are still those established by an eighteenth-century Constitution. To the extent that a Calvinist world view sanctioned such fundamental features of government as the separation of powers and checks and balances in 1787, it contributed to the tension between executive and legislative action in foreign policy which has been so manifest since 1918. While the recent pronouncements of Protestant bodies have generally sought to strengthen presidential power in treaty-making, arms control, and foreign aid and trade, they have confronted many senators and representatives from Protestant strongholds appealing to congressional prerogatives as a sacred trust assigned by the Constitution and protesting against the evils of unlimited executive power in the most Puritanical of terms. Curiously enough, the present influence of both Protestant officialdom and Catholic presidency in the 1960's is often frustrated by these appeals to the religion-shaped political decisions of the 1700's. In fact, no nation exhibits more of a founding-father complex in its political behavior. (That's the "Geyer-Freudian theory!")

Not only was the structure of constitutional government in America responsive to Calvinist influence: the very image which Americans formed of their own nation was largely shaped by that influence.

> The Puritan state was seen by Puritans as the incarnation of their collective will; it was driven by an energy they had acquired in their conversion, it was the embodied image of their power, of their resolution, of their idea. . . . New England political theory made the state almost a kind of second incarnation, a Messiah fathered by God and born of the people. Mortal men, being visited by God in the Covenant of Grace, conceive a will to moral obedience; when they covenant among themselves, when they combine their several regenerate wills into one all-inclusive will, the state becomes another savior, the child of God and man, leading men to righteousness and preparing them for the final reckoning.[12]

This incarnation doctrine of government, when placed alongside the doctrine that government must be limited because of original sin, reveals a profound internal contradiction within Puritan political thought. Government displays both a Messianic and a Satanic character. It is both a subject of sublime faith and an object of fearful contempt. The Puritans were unwilling to abandon either extreme; their politics was made to straddle the vast emotional and ethical distance between an exalted confidence and an eternal suspicion. Or, it may be said, Puritan politics bequeathed to later generations a moral pendulum which was left swinging between optimism and pessimism, between inflamed hope and dark despair. This contradiction has never been resolved within American Protestantism and continues to characterize political ethics; indeed, it remains a conspicuous feature of American political behavior generally. Americans are alternately convinced that they have the best government and the worst government. They do not consistently know whether to worship their leaders or to despise them, whether to entrust government with more responsibility or less. Many political reforms since 1898 have been products of crusaders whose moral energy derived from the judgment that government was corrupt and incompetent but whose policies prescribed an increase in government power.

Perry Miller, who has emphasized the continuing influence of Puritan ways upon national behavior, recently acknowledged to a colloquium on the American character that further research has persuaded him to modify his emphasis: the image of America since about 1815, when textile mills were opened in New England, has been that of a business civilization. This is "the dominant theme of American history." [13] Other observers claim the demise of Puritan thoughtways after 1865, or 1900, or 1920, or 1932, or 1945, or even 1960—usually under the onslaught of secular and pragmatic values. We have noted earlier, however, that millions of Americans are religious in their profession of faith and secular in their operational values. They may have acquired the worldly viewpoints of economic or occupational or sectional interests, but they cling to these temporal doctrines with Puritanical zeal. The emotional style of the Puritan ethos remains more vital than the ethical substance of it.

The moral energies of the Puritan ethos contributed to a fundamental dualism in the American character. On the one hand, they infused economic enterprise with a fervor which Max Weber and others have described as "the spirit of capitalism." On the other hand, religious life itself became fired with emotional zeal. One-hundred thirty years ago, Tocqueville identified this paradox: Americans were alternately a people of intense materialism and intense spiritualism. "Although the desire of acquiring the good things of this world is the prevailing passion of the American people, certain momentary outbreaks occur when their souls seem suddenly to burst the bonds of matter by which they are restrained and to soar impetuously toward heaven."[14] Reinhold Niebuhr suggests that this paradox is still much with us: contemporary Americans are

> at once the most religious and the most secular of Western nations. . . . We are "religious" in the sense that religious communities enjoy the devotion and engage the active loyalty of more laymen than in any nation in the Western world. We are "secular" in the sense that we pursue the immediate goals of life, without asking too many ultimate questions about the meaning of life and without being too disrupted by the tragedies and antimonies of life.[15]

The unpredictability of moral enthusiasm and the instability of public moods, as traits of American character, have engaged the attention of many contemporary writers in the field of foreign policy—notably Gabriel Almond, Hans Morgenthau, Walter Lippmann, and George Kennan. Some political scientists, however, dismiss the concept of national character entirely because of its tendency to perpetuate stereotypes. The diversity and the dynamism of American life and thought may appear more impressive than its unity or continuity. Nevertheless, the assumption of an American character is provocative of many historical and cultural questions which perhaps cannot be raised in any other way.

Traits of national character become increasingly independent of their sources. The religious qualities of the American public today bear less relationship to the intentional influences of clergymen than they once did. Religious leaders do not simply create and control religious loyalties and sentiments: their constituencies are already religious. The Puritan ethos survives more through inheritance than through indoctrination. It cuts across all denominational, ethnic, racial, sectional, and vocational boundaries. Both religious and political leaders are subject to the imperial pressures of public values shaped long before the modern period. There is that most durable doctrine which holds that faith and freedom are inseparable. President Eisenhower, on many occasions, affirmed that "free government is the political expression of a deeply-felt religious faith." Preachers and policy-makers alike testify to this providential tie between American government and American godliness. In this historic mixing of religious and political creeds and sentiments, the Puritan version of Covenant faith blended the religiosity of politicians with the politicality of the clergy.

Thus, for three centuries before 1898, the inexhaustible energies of Calvinism were storing up a religio-political force in the depths of the American character which was to be unleashed upon the world when the nation quite suddenly discovered the need for a foreign policy. All of the characteristically American responses to the modern world—in its brief and guilty imperialism, in its expeditions into foreign wars, in isolationism, pacifism, internationalism, anti-Communism—have been uttered with a Puritan accent. It is not that other nations have passed through these years without parallel responses; but American foreign policy has taken each of these modes and given a peculiarly religious zeal to it. The contradictions among them should not obscure their common source of energy in the religious components of the American character.

In the course of the nineteenth century, according to Ralph H. Gabriel, the American democratic faith had developed into a romantic, secular national religion. In part, this was to compensate for a sense of cultural inferiority to Europe. Among the doctrines of this national religion were those of the Fundamental Law, the Free Individual, and the Mission of America. It was this third doctrine which most influenced American foreign policy at the turn of the century. Exemplars of the Mission of America were: (a) Josiah Strong, whose book *Our Country* was an apology for Anglo-Saxon superiority in political and missionary imperialism: (b) Alfred Thayer Mahan, naval historian, proponent of American sea power, nationalist diplomat, and advocate of arbitration; (c) Theodore Roosevelt, who believed in

fighting for the right and in the moral duties of civilized people
to help the uncivilized; and (d) David Starr Jordan, pacifist president of Stanford University, who preached that war was contrary to both evolution and democracy.[16]

The variety of persons and viewpoints thus conditioned by a
national religion suggests that it may be misleading to picture
twentieth-century foreign policy as a dialogue between moralists
and realists, representing religious and secular groups, respectively. Public righteousness is not just a quality of religious
groups: generals, corporation presidents, and senators can quote
the Scriptures as piously as the clergy. The problem of responsible public leadership in the United States may thus be not so
much that of balancing the ethics of religious groups with the
cynicism of more secular groups: it may be that of attempting to
manage the moralistic strife among clamoring and competing
absolutists, all professing the national religion and all claiming
competence in world affairs. This problem is implicitly etched
into Brogan's portrait of the American character:

> Americans like slogans, like words. They like absolutes in
> ethics. They believe that good is good, even if they quarrel
> over what, in the circumstances, *is* good.[17]

American absolutism has been heightened by the ideological
fervor of modern politics. Twentieth-century leadership in all
nations has had to come to terms with the power of ideology.
Mass "politicization" has followed mass industrialization, mass
urbanization, mass communications, and mass education. Policy-
makers, who in the nineteenth century had to reckon primarily
with a waning aristocracy and a small if growing middle class,
have been plunged into a new relationship with a vast body
politic. How to create and manipulate mass moods which will
support government policies is a dilemma which has confronted
both totalitarian and democratic leaders. "There must be a fund
of common symbols in terms of which the loves, hates, and fears
of men, as they find public expression, are evoked, mobilized,
and discharged in similar ways. Without such a shared 'ideology'
or 'belief-system,' no government is possible."[18] Ideological dif-

ferences are as fundamental to international conflict in the twentieth century as economic competition was in the nineteenth.

This highly symbolic aspect of twentieth-century politics has provided religious and moral energies with a new access to the world arena. Religious sanctions for national policy perform precisely those functions required of a successful ideology:

> its completeness and internal coherence,
> its gorgeous vision of the future,
> its ability to hold men's imaginations,
> its pretense to provide a universal frame of
>   reference of good and evil,
> its consistency,
> its convincing criticism of the present and
>   picture of the future,
> and its ability to circumvent countercriticisms.[19]

The ideological response of American political leadership to a new age of mass ideologies—the very age in which the nation became a great power—has largely been to invoke the sanctions of its national religion. From the depths of its own historic character, the modern American nation has summoned its faith in the mission of America. The Puritan ethos cannot simply be manipulated by policy-makers, however; it is a dynamic force which may be exploited by political opposition to the government. Indeed, it has been commonly observed that American public opinion dominates foreign policy primarily in negative and *ex post facto* terms. These negative qualities of mass opinion, expressed with Puritan intensity, have engaged the continuing attention of Walter Lippmann in his writings on foreign policy. Lippmann has regarded American notions of moral superiority as a source of confusion and of international disaster.

> The rule to which there are few exceptions—the acceptance of the Marshall Plan is one of them—is that at the critical junctures, when the stakes are high, the prevailing mass opinion will impose what amounts to a veto upon changing the course on which the government is at the time proceeding. Prepare for war in time of peace? No. It is bad to raise taxes, to unbalance the budget, to take men away from their schools or their jobs, to provoke the enemy. Intervene in a develop-

ing conflict? No. Avoid the risk of war. Withdraw from the area of conflict? No. The adversary must not be appeased. Reduce your claims on the area? No. Righteousness cannot be compromised. Negotiate a compromise peace as soon as the opportunity presents itself? No. The aggressor must be punished. Remain armed to enforce the dictated settlement? No. The war is over.[20]

The American people have alternated between the indifference which is the luxury vouchsafed by a sublime confidence in Providence and a crusading zeal which is the special property of Puritanism in politics. In a detailed analysis of mass moods and their responses to a moralistic idealogy, Gabriel Almond emphasizes the instability of American "mood-simplification": now withdrawal, now intervention—now optimism, now pessimism—now idealism, now cynicism—now superiority, now inferiority. Americans tend to over-react to the problems of foreign policy. They are peculiarly capable of both overestimation and underestimation. They can shift from a broad tolerance to a narrow intolerance. While "the autonomous conscience of Puritanism" has yielded somewhat in the direction of a practical flexibility, there is a "substratum of ideological fundamentalism which frequently breaks through the surface and has an important impact on foreign policy."[21]

The American ideology thus serves two basic functions in foreign policy discussion: one positive or prescriptive, the other negative or proscriptive. These are quasi-legal functions: to legitimize certain policies and to deny legitimacy to alternative policies. The Puritan ethos is especially equipped to perform both prescriptive and proscriptive functions. Its legalism confidently attaches God's will to the "do's" and "don't's" of public behavior. Its moralistic world view has been invoked to determine whom Americans shall love and whom they shall hate and fear. The very access of public opinion to American policy gives its moral currents a political potency exceeding that of other nations. In no other great power of the twentieth century has there been as large a degree of popular control over foreign policy as there has been in the United States, and "for this reason our idealistic impulses have been allowed freer rein."[22] Puritan influence has provided more of a psychological than a logical consistency. While it has increasingly served as a mask for secular interests, the Covenant faith has provided the most characteristic expression of American foreign policy.

RELIGION AND THE POLICY-MAKER

> Whenever American statesmen and leaders have set forth their creeds and formulated the aims and goals of national policy, it has been these commonwealth principles they have enunciated. The resolve that "this nation under God shall have a new birth of freedom and that government of the people by the people and for the people shall not perish from the earth" was a resolve to preserve and perfect the American Commonwealth.[23]

Lincoln's former secretary, John Hay, asserted decades later as McKinley's Secretary of State that his policy was based on the Golden Rule.[24] At the same time, Senator Beveridge of Indiana provided an impassioned justification for imperialism: God "has made us adept in government that we may administer government among savage and senile peoples. . . . And of all our race he has marked the American people as his chosen nation to finally lead in the regeneration of the world."[25] William Jennings Bryan, thrice candidate for the Presidency and eventually Secretary of State under Wilson, was just as zealous in his opposition to imperialism, believing that the United States should seek to exercise only a moral influence in international affairs. Bryan was an eager advocate of treaties of arbitration in the early 1900's. "Throughout this period, there was no one more anti-imperialist, anti-big-Navy and anti-foreign involvement than the silver-tongued orator who preached to a thousand Chautauqua audiences on 'The Prince of Peace.' "[26] With Josiah Strong, Alfred Thayer Mahan, Theodore Roosevelt, and David Starr Jordan, these men believed in "the mission of America"—although they could not agree as to just what that mission should be or how it should be carried out.

The sincerity of some such utterances may be questioned.

In the United States, there tends to be a religious angle to all fundamental policies. Religious sentiments have cohesive power: presidents, secretaries of state, and other public figures continually play upon religious themes to create a focus for popular loyalties. Thus religious influence is not simply to be controlled by religious leaders themselves: it is subject to manipulation by anyone having access to mass opinion, whether politicians, advertisers, journalists, or educators. The American public is vulnerable to anything with a religious label: there is a

> well-publicized notion that religion is a form of social and psychological therapy; that it is a bulwark against Communism, juvenile delinquency, family instability, and the hydrogen bomb; that it should be the basis for foreign policy and national legislative goals. It is possible that these sentiments stem from genuine concern about pressing problems or from an interest in achieving a wider recognition for the religious orientation; but their cumulative effect can be divisive and, under crisis conditions, they may foster the acceptance of illusory solutions to grave problems. Popular religion lends itself to ideological manipulation and, thus, religion is often invoked in the effort to obtain non-religious ends, that is, as an instrument of political and public policy.[27]

It is perhaps more than accidental that the two American statesmen of the twentieth century who may be regarded as the purest political products of Puritanism—Woodrow Wilson and John Foster Dulles—were preoccupied with the power of mass opinion. Before them, Theodore Roosevelt had mixed the image of Calvin with that of the cowboy, giving the Presidency the moral force of both: he was always staging "the breathless drama of a Western movie, and he never left the audience in doubt that he was the 'good guy' and the other fellows—Democrats, senators, monopolists, Socialists, diplomats, nature fakers, muckrakers—the 'bad guys.' " It is Rossiter's judgment that Roosevelt "was a brilliant molder and interpreter of public opinion, who confessed happily that the White House was a 'bully pulpit.' " [28]

It was left to Woodrow Wilson, however, to exploit the moral power of the Presidency to the full. One of the most unintended and ironic consequences of the American Constitution, in its reaction to monarchy and its separation of powers, was to prepare the way for a modern presidency which would overshadow both the monarchs and the prime ministers of the twentieth century. The moral power of the office in an age of ideology and mass nationalism was enhanced by the very combination of the symbolic functions of chief of state with the political authority of the chief executive. Moreover, while the removal of the chief executive from membership in the parliamentary body was intended to reduce his power over that body, it had the potential effect of providing the President with a privileged sanctuary in the White House whose "bully pulpit" did not require a daily defense before Congress. And, finally, the popular voting for the Presidency was to afford the holder of that office an opportunity to claim a mandate for national action which prime ministers must always be prepared to win anew with parliamentary votes of confidence. In combining the majesty of a king with the power of a prime minister, the Constitution made it possible for an American President to feel that "all his powers are invigorated, indeed are given a new dimension of authority, because he is the symbol of our sovereignty, continuity, and grandeur."[29]

Wilson perceived this historic development long before he became its embodiment. In 1908, he had written of the symbolic power of the President:

> The nation as a whole has chosen him, and is conscious that it has no other political spokesman. His is the only national voice in affairs. Let him once win the admiration and confidence of the country, and no other single force can withstand him, no combination of forces will easily overpower him. His position takes the imagination of the country. He is the representative of no constituency, but of the whole people. When he speaks in his true character, he speaks of no special interest. If he rightly interpret the national thought and boldly insist upon it, he is irresistible, and the country never feels the zest of action so much as when its president is of such insight and caliber. Its instinct is for unified action, and it craves a single leader.[30]

Wilson's appeal for open diplomacy and his rousing response

from mass opinion in both Europe and America were striking anticipations of the more recent years of ideological warfare and of the United Nations as what Herman Finer has called a forum "for the mobilization of shame." A student of public opinion has said of Wilson: "His general knowledge of the character and thought of the people and their historical tendencies coupled with an almost uncanny ability to sense the aspirations of the people seems to have accounted for his ability to crystallize public opinion and express the common feeling in clear and striking fashion." [31]

The zest for action which Wilson brought to the Presidency and which the masses were made to feel through him is commonly attributed by both Wilson's critics and his defenders to his Calvinistic background. Wilson's moral interests—in covenant style—were articulated with a combination of exalted nationalism and missionary internationalism to which the American public typically responded with enthusiasm: "We have an object lesson to give to the rest of the world." "The idea of America is to serve humanity." "We are the mediating nation." "The force of America is the force of moral principle." He regarded the Covenant of the League of Nations as the universal fulfillment of the American covenant, its Constitution.

Wilson's critics have claimed that his Calvinistic background made him an uncompromising idealist who was largely responsible for the failure of the United States to subscribe to the Covenant of his League. If he had only been willing to compromise with Henry Cabot Lodge's reservations, it is said, American acceptance of the Covenant would have been made politically possible. Blum contends that "the politics of morality" practiced by Wilson offended the leaders of other nations and alienated potential support at home. "A fervid legalism, then a missionary constitutionalism tinged with racialism, a sentimental pacifism shaped Wilson's foreign policy." [32]

Wilson's defenders recognize the power of the same religious influences upon his leadership and profess to see in him the manifestation of the true American character and its mission in the world. Norman Cousins rejects the patronizing skepticism with which it became fashionable in the twenties and thirties to view Wilson's idealism:

> Wilson was perhaps the most practical man of his time, for he had addressed himself to the basic needs of America and the world. . . . He was representing the strength of America as he understood it and as history had confirmed it. We do not honor his memory unless we also honor his convictions. At the heart of those convictions was the belief that vision—vision with spaciousness and moral grandeur—is not only the solvent of potential danger but the natural setting for a human community at peace.[33]

Notwithstanding the failure of the League, Wilson had provided the most radical redefinition of American foreign policy since the Monroe Doctrine and had charted the main directions of the American response to international conflict for a half-century: the quest for a peaceful international order and collective defense against aggression.

The most authentic diplomatic heir to President Wilson was Secretary of State John Foster Dulles. Dulles, too, was the son of a Presbyterian clergyman. One of his grandfathers was a missionary, the other a Secretary of State. Dulles attended Princeton during Wilson's university presidency. Originally inclined to the ministry, he decided for law and diplomacy, first attaining national recognition as one of Wilson's principal advisers at Versailles. However, his most conspicuous platform for foreign policy views prior to becoming Dewey's adviser and Eisenhower's Secretary of State was afforded by the churches. Dulles was a delegate to the Oxford Conference on Church, State, and Community in 1937. In 1940, he was appointed chairman of the Federal Council of Churches' Commission on a Just and Durable Peace which, during the war, he used to win mass support for the United Nations—believing finally that this campaign had made the difference between 1919 (the campaign which Wilson was unable to finish) and 1945 in public support for international organization. In 1946, at Cambridge, he was instrumental in the creation of the Commission of the Churches on International Affairs (CCIA), jointly sponsored by the International Missionary

Council and the World Council of Churches. At the Amsterdam Assembly of the World Council in 1948, Dulles declared:

> What seems urgent—and possible—is to revive in men a sense of moving peacefully toward a state of greater perfection. . . . The need is for more effective political use of moral power. . . . The Christian churches are especially qualified to help men form moral judgments which are discerning and to focus them at the time and place where they can be effective. The need is for full use of the present great possibilities of the United Nations. It was Christians most of all who wanted a world organisation which would depend primarily on moral rather than physical power. They have it. Now it is up to the churches to generate the moral power required to make the organisation work.[34]

The fact that Dulles continued, after 1948, to be a spokesman for bipartisan internationalism in American foreign policy did not for him preclude the assertion of a vigorous nationalism. He drafted the foreign policy plank of the Republican platform in 1952:

> The present administration, in seven years, has squandered the unprecedented power and prestige which were ours at the close of World War II. In that time, more than 500,000,000 non-Russian people of 15 different countries have been absorbed into the power sphere of Communist Russia, which proceeds confidently with its plan for world conquest. We charge that the leaders of the administration in power lost the peace so dearly earned by World War II.[35]

Just as the Wilson administration had been obsessed with loyalty investigations in its late months, the Dulles tenure at the State Department began in the full tide of Senator McCarthy's loyalty investigations, to which Dulles was responsive. The first press release of the new Secretary, the day after President Eisenhower's inauguration, sternly insisted upon the virtue of loyalty:

> We are front-line defenders of the vital interests of the United States which are being attacked by a political warfare which is as hostile in its purpose and as dangerous in its capabilities as any open war. . . . The peril is of a kind which places a special responsibility on each and every member of the Department of State and the Foreign Service. It requires of us

competence, discipline, and positive loyalty to the policies
that our President and the Congress may prescribe. Less than
that is not tolerable at this time. . . . I know, and our fellow
citizens know, that those who comprise the Department of
State and Foreign Service are, as a whole, a group of loyal
Americans dedicated to the preservation of American ideals.[36]

This proclamation of the Puritan ideals of "competence, discipline, and positive loyalty" had political overtones which were
demoralizing to career men in the Department and in the Foreign Service, a number of whom resigned or were "retired."[37]
But, whatever its consequences for the administration of American foreign policy, it reflected Dulles' pronounced sensitivity to
the symbols of the American ideology and to mass opinion. While
statements by a Secretary of State have ordinarily taken account
of home consumption aspects, the greater care has normally been
given to the conveying of American policy to other governments;
domestic impact has been a secondary consideration. Dulles reversed this emphasis. It was his theory that foreign policy, no
matter how wise and sound, could not succeed in a democratic
republic unless the mass of people understood it and supported
it. It was his conviction that his first job as Secretary in 1953 was
"to restore the American public's confidence in the State Department."[38]

Woodrow Wilson and John Foster Dulles—two devout Presbyterians—brought to the foreign policy of five decades a renewed projection, in bold relief, of the Puritan ethos. One important clue to their public behavior is that each incarnated the
internal tension inherent in the doctrine of the covenant: a
"chosen people" is at once zealously nationalistic and zealously
universalistic. Each generated a missionary internationalism in
his time; each invoked the most earnest sanctions upon national
loyalty. Each was a preacher as well as a policy-maker, seeking
to win mass support for his convictions.

In their political leadership, Wilson and Dulles exhibited
both the cohesive and divisive properties of religion itself. Because each was perceived by the public to be a special embodiment of the national religion, he won a vast, enthusiastic, un-

critical following for a time. But the covenant tension is difficult to maintain. Wilson's success as an internationalist was not matched by his last political efforts as a nationalist. Dulles had the opposite trouble: his success as a nationalist finally weakened his impact as a world statesman.

In the days of their sovereign hold on public opinion, the American people found in Wilson and Dulles (to use Weber's term) an "elective affinity" between their intensely held doctrine of the mission of America and the political requirements of foreign policy. Tawney has written of the Puritan Revolution in England:

> There is a magic mirror in which each order and organ of society, as the consciousness of its character and destiny dawns upon it, looks for a moment, before the dust of conflict or the glamour of success obscures its vision. . . . For the middle classes of the early seventeenth century, rising but not yet triumphant, that enchanted mirror was Puritanism.[39]

Three centuries later, when an increasingly middle-class America was called upon for its first responsible foreign policy in generations of revolutionary conflict; when the very nature of the conflict lifted ideology above economics; when the depths of the nation's character and destiny were to be portrayed before a world arena, the "magic mirror" was much the same. Diluted and manipulated by secular influences it may have become—but the Puritan ethos has given Americans their most distinctive vision of their role in international affairs. Unstable and inconsistent may be the part played—the very instabilities and inconsistencies dramatize Puritan action. Both the feats and the failures of United States foreign policy must be seen in that mirror.

RELIGION
AS A SANCTION FOR CONFLICT

POLITICAL CONFLICT AS A RELIGIOUS DUTY

The third function of religion in world politics is to interpret political conflict as a religious obligation. The Psalmist sang of God's help in time of hostilities:

> He trains my hands for war,
>   so that my arms can bend a bow of bronze. . . .
> For thou didst gird me with strength for the battle;
>   thou didst make my assailants sink under me.
> Thou didst make my enemies turn their backs to me,
>   and those who hated me I destroyed.[1]

The prophets heard the judgments of God proclaimed in international conflict, whether as vindication or as punishment for the people of the Covenant. Jesus warned: "Do not think that I have come to bring peace on earth: I have not come to bring peace, but a sword."[2] His vision of the future was that of "wars and rumors of wars. . . . For nation will rise up against nation, and kingdom against kingdom."[3] Jesus found more faith in a Roman centurion than he found among his own people.[4] He told the multitudes that the cost of discipleship had to be counted with the same calculating wisdom with which a king prepared to wage war.[5]

If these texts cannot dictate a simple answer to the ethical dilemmas of war and peace, they do belong to a vast body of scriptural teaching which accepts the realities of hostility and violence and announces the will of God as active in and through such realities. Scriptural symbols have been conspicuous in the most violent conflicts of Western history:

> For the past sixteen hundred years, the cross and the sword have been symbolic of Christendom. Ever since Constantine discovered military value in the unifying ideal of loyalty to the cross, and made it a sign under which his legions fought, the Church has been a participant in war. Battle flags have been displayed in cathedrals, Popes have called the faithful to crusades against the infidel with sword and lance and crossbow, bishops have blessed the hosts of imperialism and have sent forth troops and navies to fight against primitive peoples for purposes of enslavement, with pious benedictions. It has been the aim of national governments to secure the full co-operation of the Church in time of war, and with few exceptions that co-operation has been obtained.[6]

SUPPORT FOR INTERNATIONAL CONFLICT

As the power of the church tended to decline in the face of modern nationalism, the church's role with regard to war was modified. Toynbee has set apart the eighteenth century as a period of civilized warfare marked by the waning influence of religion but prior to the full emergence of nationalism. "The fundamental reason why war was less atrocious in the eighteenth century than either before or since was that it had ceased to be a weapon of religious fanaticism and had not yet become a weapon of nationalist fanaticism."[7]

Nationalist fanaticism has reached its peak in the twentieth century. Statesmen have learned that mass opinion must be aroused to moral indignation against the enemies of the nation if a total war is to be waged. Religious zeal has been courted by political leaders as a power uniquely capable of generating moral indignation. "No national government could ever secure a more powerful organ of propaganda than a church quickening moral indignation against the enemy of the moment, and doing it on information which, as the crisis deepens, is more definitely controlled, more carefully filtered out to the country, by the agencies of the home government itself."[8] This whipping up of moral indignation into a "war for righteousness" is "the clue to the deadliest features of modern war—the hatred, the viciousness, the refusal to compromise."[9]

Historians of American foreign policy testify to the manner in which the Puritan ethos has generated the moral indignation of the nation's modern wars. George Kennan's criticism of American moralism repeatedly calls attention to the way in which that trait has driven national policy to punitive extremes such as the demand for unconditional surrender. "It is a curious thing," Kennan reflects, that moralism, "rooted as it unquestionably is in a desire to do away with war and violence, makes violence more enduring, more terrible, and more destructive to political stability than did the older motives of national interest. A war fought in the name of high moral principle finds no early end short of some form of total domination."[10] Historic circumstances have helped to accentuate this punitive note in American sentiment: the public responded with an explosive conviction of outrage to the sinking of the *Maine* in 1898, the submarine attacks of 1917, and the bombing of Pearl Harbor in 1941.

There tends to be a vicious circle of moral fervor and acute guilt. The very intensity of participation by many religious persons in conflict is a function of guilt and insecurity feelings over having taken such positions. When the moral restraints against violence are relaxed so that the full power of moral indignation may be released, the resolution of the conflict becomes more difficult to achieve. "Ideological conflict is more intense and the parties thereto are more intransigent because of the objectification of issues and lack of inhibitions on personal attacks."[11] After hostilities cease and moral enthusiasms are spent, guilt lingers and disillusionment follows. The sustained moral effort required by policies for an effective peace is then doubly difficult to produce.

The horrors of war should not blind us to the fact that war is a very satisfying experience in some respects: it serves positive functions. The deeper psychic functions of religion in sanctioning war are suggested by J. C. Flugel's analysis of the psychological appeals of war. Among these appeals are: (1) adventure: the zest for the unknown, the demand on bodily and mental powers, the fascination of risk and danger, the need to sacrifice (or to punish the self); (2) social unity: the experience of common emotions and purposes as the idea of the nation becomes vivid and powerful; co-operation, the lifting of the ego to the super-ego, the "need to be needed"; (3) freedom from individual worries and restrictions: submerging of the individual to the common danger, reduction of economic worry through employment security, reduction of class and status distinctions, relaxing of moral inhibitions; and (4) aggression: the availability of an enemy as a scapegoat and the reduction of domestic aggression. War serves as an "outlet for moralized aggression. . . . As a means of doing evil and of feeling good while doing it, war is without a parallel."[12] Perhaps no agency is better equipped to moralize or justify these psychological appeals of war than the church. Its own preaching of sacrifice, co-operation, peace of mind, and moral indignation seems to afford the church a special appropriateness in times of national crisis, including war. The fact that the costs of nuclear war are intolerable both ethically and politically demands of religious leaders a most imaginative effort to provide what William James called a "moral equivalent of war."

After the sinking of the U. S. battleship *Maine* in Havana Harbor on February 15, 1898, Protestant clergy became especially vociferous in demanding a war policy. Their bellicosity had already been unwittingly warmed by another kind of war: a circulation war between the Hearst and Pulitzer papers in New York which had resulted in the fabrication or exaggeration of many accounts of Spanish atrocities. Thus did "yellow journalism" maneuver Protestant influence into a policy of imperialism, although Spanish responsibility for the sinking of the *Maine* was never proved and notwithstanding a Spanish willingness to negotiate. With the inauguration of hostilities by the McKinley administration in late April, the editor of *The Methodist Review* declared: "We shall be much disappointed if the final outcome of the war does not show that it was one of God's most efficient agencies for the advancement of true Christian civilization and the ushering in of brighter times for the human race."[13]

Another reason for Protestant enthusiasm for the war was the prospect of new missionary activity in the Orient where Catholic missions had predominated. This was an element in the final decision of McKinley himself. The President, before making up his mind, told Methodist leaders that he often went down on his knees "and prayed Almighty God for light and guidance." His invalid wife had a zealous concern for "the heathen of the Philippines." After the decision was made, Mc-Kinley announced that there was no alternative but "to take them all, and educate the Filipinos, and uplift and civilize them, and by God's grace to do the very best we could for them, as our fellow men for whom Christ also died."[14]

In the summer of 1900, a second imperialistic policy was proclaimed with a pious ring: the "Open Door" for China to guarantee the territorial and administrative integrity of that country against Western dismemberment. A less conspicuous motive was the promotion of American trade in the Far East. The "Open Door" was vigorously supported by American church leaders and missionary interests. Public opinion was persuaded that a righteous covenant had been contracted with the imperialists—those *other* countries—even though the policy failed of any significant practical result. The United States was unwilling to back its own commitment in any forceful way, and Secretary of State Hay himself became disillusioned by the policy. An exhortatory policy may thus win public support among the American people, especially if supported by the churches, at the same time that it alienates and embarrasses allies and fails to safeguard the interests of the very people for whom the nation has expressed moral concern:

> Time after time we would call upon other powers to make public confession of these principles. Time after time we would receive from them reluctant, evasive, or qualified replies, putting us on notice that no one would deny the principles but that it all depended on how they were interpreted. Time after time we would present these replies to our own people, despite their qualified nature, as diplomatic achievements: as acknowledgments of the justice of our view, expressions of contrition, willingness to reform.[15]

After the outbreak of war in Europe in 1914, Britain and France addressed moral appeals to Americans, encouraging their enlistment in a crusade against the immoral Germans. Woodrow Wilson's policy of neutrality was at first supported by the churches, which had launched a variety of peace movements in the early 1900's. When Lyman Abbott and other church leaders joined the efforts of the Security League in zealously pushing for war and allowed themselves to become instruments of Allied propaganda, it became possible for peace enthusiasts to redirect their energies. On the Monday after the United States broke diplomatic relations with Germany in February, American newspapers reported a large number of Sunday sermons advocating intervention. Wilson himself, still not decided upon a declaration of war, declared: "I think our clergy have all gone crazy."[16] While Wilson's own reluctance was eventually converted to enthusiasm, that enthusiasm was more a product of a clamoring public opinion than its producer. The prewar weeks of 1917 witnessed a milling process in which both Wilson and the general public were subject to pressures which, in the end, they could not withstand.

The churches finally pitched into the war effort with the unrestrained fervor of a crusade. Frank Mason North, president of the Federal Council of Churches, proclaimed: "The war for righteousness will be won! Let the Church do her part." Protestant leaders turned their churches into "little more than government agencies carrying out the will of the state." They recruited soldiers, sold Liberty bonds, saved food, and urged the raising of production quotas. Sermons were preached "from outlines sent them by government propaganda agencies," especially for the playing up of atrocities by Germans and in exposing plots and spies. The clergy agitated for the curtailment of civil liberties; the Wilson administration made haste to accommodate them. The I.W.W., German-Americans, conscientious objectors, and pacifists were all "lumped together for widespread ministerial denunciation and condemnation."[17] In this mood, *Zion's Herald* —later to manifest a passion for peace—announced: "God's employment of War as a means of dispensing with useless and harmful material is too conspicuous a feature of Scripture to allow standing room to Quakers and men with a quaking disposition."[18]

In a brilliant recent commentary on the consequences of the war of 1914-1918, George Kennan has lamented the total self-righteousness with which the war was waged—not only at the cost of immense suffering and tragedy for many nations, but also to the point where any rational political objectives were lost in the hysteria. Lord Lansdowne's letter, published in late 1917, pleaded for an early end of hostilities on the basis of compromise with Germany rather than unconditional surrender. Lansdowne, a distinguished Conservative diplomat and a devoted patriot who wrote from the depths of personal suffering and sadness, issued what Kennan terms "one of the most moving and penetrating documents of our time." The Allies rejected the letter out of hand, with the result that the first World War became "*the* great catastrophe of Western civilization in the present century."[19] The relentless prosecution of the war not only added countless casualties: it issued in a peace treaty at Versailles which would help to generate those forces in the German body politic which Adolf Hitler would manipulate so shrewdly in coming years, and it provoked a bitterness between the Allies and the leaders of the Russian Revolution which was never subsequently to be healed.

Disillusionment and guilt came swiftly after the Armistice— and the churches were vitally affected. While some religious leaders sought to rally a new crusade for peace, the churches themselves were losing membership and influence. Protestant denominations generally experienced a "severe decline in prestige and popular appeal because of their war record. The accusation that they had abandoned their pacific mission, blessed the arms of all belligerents and exhorted their respective uniformed flocks to exterminate one another as a sacred, religious duty carried the more conviction as indeed far too many churchmen of all denominations had surrendered to the war psychosis."[20] Bailey proposes a "political law of gravitation" according to which the reaction to intense moral fervor may be described:

"The higher the idealism the greater the subsequent disillusionment. There is a corollary law: a nation is able to key itself up to a high pitch for only a relatively short time, and then reaction sets in."[21]

The reaction to World War I eventually gave a renewed strength to pacifism in the churches and made for qualitative differences in the response of Protestantism to World War II. Tempered also by the growing solidarity and the theological seriousness of a world ecumenical movement which transcended the boundaries of all belligerents, churches tended to hold aloof from the excesses of frenzy during World War II. There was more of an attitude of resignation to the reality of aggression and less disposition to whip up hate for the Huns. There was a wider concern for civil liberties and for the treatment of conscientious objectors. Lasswell describes American sentiments in 1941-1945 as "a struggle to stop a sadistic gang of thugs, but it was done without enthusiasm, without an overwhelming sense of mission. Somehow the whole business seemed a side issue in a world where there are major issues." Public opinion had been drained of its capacity for moral revulsion and had become increasingly callous to the brutalities of international violence.[22] The momentum of total war first justified obliteration bombing by conventional bombs, then rationalized the atomic attacks upon Hiroshima and Nagasaki.

Batchelder's recent inquiry into that "irreversible decision" concludes that only a small minority of the American people was disturbed by the dropping of atom bombs. Although the decision was made in secret and represented a failure of political imagination, it did not prove to be contrary to the spiritual climate which had developed during the course of the war. "Churchmen proved only slightly more resistant than political leaders to this erosion of moral principles."[23] The absolutes of unconditional surrender and military necessity closed the door "on a whole series of opportunities, any one of which might have made a difference, and which, taken all together, probably would have resulted in an outcome different from that which actually occurred—the killing of more than 100,000 people, and the crossing of the barrier into the dangerous world where a precedent exists for the military use of atomic energy."[24] Nothing accounts more for the apparent defensiveness of American policy in the field of atomic weapons since 1945 than the rationalization of those first attacks; one of the weakest spots in American political armor against Communist propaganda is the fact that we have used the bomb and they haven't.

The lack of substantial religious protest against the bomb produced its own international repercussions. Braden reported that Hiroshima was a great shock to the people of India, but

> even more shocking was the rationalization of its use by the Bishops and religious leaders of the West—not all of them, of course, for there were exceptions. . . . It seemed the ultimate in the repudiation of the principles of the Christian faith and did irreparable harm to that faith in India. It appeared to millions, particularly of the followers of Gandhi, as something monstrous in the extreme.[25]

Japan's own experience of the holocaust of the bomb combined with the de-militarization drive of the American occupation to inscribe an official pacifism into the MacArthur Constitution: the Japanese people "forever renounce war as a sovereign right of the nation and the threat or use of force as means of settling international disputes." When the United States and Japan negotiated a mutual defense assistance agreement in 1954, Japanese Christians and others protested that the agreement was unconstitutional.

If there was less moral fervor in the American public in 1941-1945 than in 1917-1918 and more discriminating judgment by some religious leaders, Protestantism generally supported the war and its goal of unconditional surrender: a goal which, as we have seen, has been sharply questioned by students of diplomacy. The retreat from pacifism and the sanctioning of the military conduct of the war manifested the pervasive involvement of American Protestantism in the society of which it is a part and the identification of religious leaders with the "mission of America."

Charles A. Eaton, former Baptist clergyman who had responded with particular zeal to the war of 1917 and who had become chairman of the House Committee on Foreign Affairs in the Republican Eightieth Congress, declared in 1947:

> Americans are such good people that they are slow to recognize wickedness. . . . Compromise with Russia seems impossible. . . . They have no morals and no religion. . . . Russians are Slavs, which means captives or slaves. . . . But we still have the atomic bomb. . . . Once kicked out of decent society, Russia must either seek to regain good standing or be disciplined by the military action of the union of decent nations.[26]

Thus was the moral indignation of a new crusade unleashed in the second year after the surrender of Germany and Japan—in response to a new militancy on the part of our recent ally, the Soviet Union. Increasingly, the demonology of Communism played upon both Catholic and Protestant fears. Catholics were most bitter about the loss of countries in eastern Europe; Protestants were shocked by the fall of China, a country in which they had invested so much—that event may yet prove to be the most enormous single disaster in this century. These tragedies abroad were exploited in partisan struggles at home. By 1950, Senator Joseph McCarthy of Wisconsin became the most hypnotic crusading orator in the country because he was able to manipulate a growing national indignation over Communist intransigence and aggression. McCarthy proclaimed that Communist successes were really the fault of Communists in the State Department—although not a single proven Communist could be found there when the Eisenhower administration took office in January, 1953.

The ideological intensity of the American-Russian conflict was personally dramatized in the policies and the language of John Foster Dulles after 1952. In the Republican platform of that year, he had called for a new policy of liberation to

> mark the end of the negative, futile, and immoral policy of "containment" which abandons countless human beings to a despotism and Godless terrorism which in turn enables the rulers to forge the captives into a weapon for our destruction. . . . The policies we espouse will revive the contagious, liberating influences which are inherent in freedom. They will in-

evitably set up strains and stresses within the captive world which will make the rulers impotent to continue in their monstrous ways and mark the beginning of their end. Our nation will again become the dynamic, moral, and spiritual force which was the despair of despots and the hope of the oppressed.[27]

The author of the containment policy, George Kennan, had been generally regarded as the nation's foremost Russian expert when Dulles became Secretary of State.[28] In early 1953, Kennan, a Foreign Service officer, was in Washington awaiting reassignment after having been recalled from his ambassadorship to Moscow at Russian insistence. Dulles, by not arranging for Kennan's reassignment, secured his automatic retirement. (Kennan returned to diplomatic duty in 1961 as President Kennedy's ambassador to Yugoslavia.) In this connection, it is important to recall that Kennan had also by 1953 become the most persistent professional critic of the influences of moralism upon American diplomacy; that he was temperamentally at odds with the Puritan zeal which Dulles so clearly manifested; that Dulles regarded Kennan as a political liability to the new administration; and that, several years later, Kennan was to advance a proposal for a policy of disengagement of American and Soviet spheres of influence, the polar opposite of Dullesian liberation. Faced with an opportunity to practice liberation in backing the Hungarian revolution of 1956 with American force, Eisenhower and Dulles declined to do so because of the risk of nuclear war. The Kennan policy of containment was more or less reinstated—without public announcement.

The Calvinist zest for action with which Dulles and other policy-makers have prosecuted the ideological struggle against the Communists is partly a cause and partly a consequence of the zest of the Communists themselves. Butterfield makes the parallel explicit: "If Communism is revolutionary, it hardly exceeds sixteenth-century Calvinism in its energy as a militant, missionary, expanding creed. As the headquarters of international revolution, the Geneva of Calvin presents important features which make it a remarkable anticipation of modern times." [29] It is precisely the religious zeal of the Communists which poses such a formidable challenge to the national religion of Americans. That Marxism is atheistic should not obscure the fact that it serves as a creed pretending to meet the ultimate problems of life. If the Puritan ethos has contributed a Messianic compound of nationalism and internationalism to the American body politic, it confronts the same qualities in its great world antagonist.

This "mutual Messianism" of the Cold War is fraught with special dangers. One such danger is the inability to analyze or comprehend Communism itself with rational clarity. Most Americans, whether in their frenzy or in their apathy (these are not necessarily contradictory traits), have failed to make a thorough, patient, systematic study of Communism, its philosophy, its literature, and its history. It takes less effort just to be *against* Communism and go on with one's private pleasures. Anti-Communist fervor often masks the moral and intellectual immaturity of persons who will not really make the effort to understand either what they oppose or what they affirm.

A second danger is that this negativism tends to drain American influence of its own positive witness in the world arena. There is a disposition to enlist every non-Communist nation, whatever its own ideology, in the struggle of the so-called Free World against atheistic Communism. Fascist and feudalistic regimes on four continents have been protected by the umbrella of the *Pax Americana,* thus unwittingly providing the Communists with their most formidable strategic advantage in the ideological conflict: the moral initiative. It is incredible to many Americans that their nation should often seem to be the enemy of social change in a revolutionary world—such is their own revolutionary heritage. The Communists welcome every opportunity to parade as the paragons of the world's future and to portray the United States as a fearful and reactionary regime clinging to the past.

Yet another hazard is to distract moral energies from chronic domestic problems which threaten our own institutions and which sap American influence abroad. A "Christian anti-Communist crusade" enlists many persons who would rather not face the hard tasks of resolving racial tensions, battling for better education, or revitalizing blighted cities. It takes no political or moral courage to be against Communism in the United States: it often takes vast reservoirs of courage to be against race segregation, or against a low salary-scale for public school teachers which can only be raised by higher taxes, or against a real estate combine which blocks or exploits an urban renewal program. In fact, anti-Communist fervor has all too often been manipulated by narrow interests to channel hostilities against those who are most loyal to the spirit of liberty, as Judge Learned Hand conceived it: the "spirit of an America which has never been, and which may never be; nay, which never will be except as the conscience and courage of Americans create it."

The most serious danger of all lurks behind an unprecedented dilemma for American statesmanship: how to rekindle a sense of national purpose at the same time that new restraints upon moral fervor must be developed. In the years of the United States' most massive power, it has at last been confronted by a rival which has developed a Puritanical zeal of its own. The Communists have stolen much of the moral thunder of the democracies—they have contrived their own ways of unleashing moral indignation as a weapon of the Cold War. Political ignorance, ideological negativism, domestic stagnation in the American public all increase the totalitarian potential of the world's one last war to which "mutual Messianism" could lead the human race. As Butterfield sees it,

> The greatest menace to our civilization today is the conflict between giant organized systems of self-righteousness—each system only too delighted to find that the other is wicked—each only too glad that the sins give it the pretext for still deeper hatred and animosity. The effect of the whole situation is barbarizing, since both sides take the wickedness of the other as the pretext for insults, atrocities, and loathing; and each side feels that its own severities are not vicious at all, but simply punitive acts and laudable measures of judgment.[30]

A hopeful note is sounded by some American observers of Russian affairs who detect a waning of ideological zeal in the

Soviet Union as new classes of complacent artists, scientists, and bureaucrats become less and less willing to jeopardize their private satisfactions in the violence of a relentless revolution.

SUPPORT FOR DOMESTIC CONFLICT

There is a domestic diplomacy as well as an international diplomacy: it has to do with the political context of foreign policy, not only in Washington and in the political parties but in every community and in every substantial interest group. In this political context, domestic hostilities may reflect international loyalties and conflicts. Religious groups may sanction domestic political conflict through identification with various ethnic groups, publics, and political parties.

For many Americans, national loyalty has been somewhat ambiguous: there remain ties of sentiment with the old country which frequently affect attitudes toward United States foreign policy. Because denominational differences tend both to reflect and perpetuate these diverse national origins, religious influence upon public opinion at times is more a matter of ethnic influence. Thus Episcopalians were more in sympathy with England and with the idea of American intervention in 1914-1917 than were Lutherans, who showed marked German sympathies until war was actually declared, whereupon Lutherans seemed to be most anxious to prove how patriotic they could be. Thus Catholic priests and editors supported Irish freedom with incomparable fidelity until that cause was won in 1921, and the same were generally isolationist when the issues of intervention against Italy and Germany were being discussed in the 1930's. Lubell indicates that Catholic militancy in the anti-Communist movements is, in part, a matter of over-compensation for the inferior social status associated with late immigration: the crusade against Communism "is almost the first political cause which has given Catholics generally the chance to feel more American than other Americans." [31] The identification of the majority of American Jews with the cause of Zionism is a force to be reckoned with in United States policy concerning Israel and the Middle East.

Conflicting patriotisms may thus be reflected in religious lobbies and voting blocs on some sensitive foreign policy issues. The slowing down of immigration and the weakening of denominational boundaries in America's mobile middle class have combined to homogenize Protestant attitudes increasingly in the past two generations.

There are no specifically Catholic or Protestant parties in the United States as there are in western Europe. Any attempt to organize such a party would surely meet public repudiation and failure. Moreover, informal attempts to identify religion with a particular party have been hotly resented by both religious and political leaders. Reinhold Niebuhr and a committee of one hundred clergymen charged the Republicans in 1956 with attempting to claim the sanctions of Christianity for the campaign to re-elect President Eisenhower. In 1960, the Catholic affiliation of Senator John F. Kennedy brought statements from leaders of all faiths that religion should not be the criterion for partisan voting.

These efforts to keep religion out of politics have not always been successful. Differences among Protestant denominations according to voting behavior normally tend, however, to reflect the social and economic status of the denominations rather than cohesive blocs. Thus Presbyterians and Episcopalians correlate more highly with Republican voting than do Baptists or Methodists—but Presbyterians and Episcopalians more generally represent upper class categories of income, occupation, and education. Religious affiliation is normally a latent cross-pressure exerting only minor influence nationally within the total Protestant electorate.[32] Not all foreign policy issues touch class status or economic interests directly, however. Presbyterians, Episcopalians, and Congregationalists, notwithstanding their economic conservatism, tend to be more internationalist on foreign policy matters than do Methodists, Lutherans, or Baptists.[33] But here again, we are only noting correlations, not organized voting blocs which necessarily come into conflict.

The pattern is quite different with regard to Jews. Consistent liberalism, internationalism, and Democratic party support have characterized Jewish voters since 1936—a pattern which has cut across all lines of status and class. Fuchs attributes such behavior to the long, bitter history of the Jews as a persecuted people battling for international security and human rights.[34] The political attachment of Jews to Franklin Roosevelt was recorded in overwhelming support at the polls—an attachment which neither Truman nor Dewey could match in 1948. Not that they didn't try during the Middle East crisis which preceded:

> If the Arabs had the oil, which was far away, the American Jews had the vote, which was near at hand, and the latter might, especially in New York, turn the forthcoming election against Harry S. Truman. With an obvious play for votes, but much to the annoyance of the British, both President Truman and his prospective opponent, Governor Thomas E. Dewey of New York, urged Britain in 1946 to admit a minimum of 100,000 Jews to Palestine.[35]

Whatever the motives of Truman and Dewey, the 1948 election found Jews a people with a new country but without a party. Jews were alienated from both major parties, many voting for Henry Wallace and many refusing to vote altogether. While a majority apparently voted for Truman after all, the bloc pattern was temporarily shattered. Lubell tells of a large Jewish family in Brooklyn which had voted solidly for F.D.R. in 1940, but which tallied this way in 1948: Truman (11), Wallace (8), Norman Thomas (1), stayed home (1). "I registered," the last-mentioned explained, "and must have changed my mind half a dozen times, but just finally gave up." [36]

In 1952, as both Catholics and Protestants were responsive to the Eisenhower crusade and to Dulles' liberation pledge, Jews resumed their strong attachment to the Democratic Party. Adlai Stevenson's defense of civil liberties and articulate internationalism won him 77 per cent of the Jewish vote. During the continuing Middle East turmoil of the 1950's, Jewish leaders were sharply critical of the Eisenhower administration for its alleged pro-Arab policies and "oil politics." Stevenson again

received more than 75 per cent of Jewish votes as Eisenhower
was winning by a landslide in 1956.

The 1960 campaign was dominated by two issues which
touched religious and moral sensitivities deeply: the Catholic
affiliation of Senator John F. Kennedy and the public preoccupation with American prestige abroad. Vice-President
Richard M. Nixon succeeded in holding 62 per cent of the
Protestant vote (Eisenhower had received 63 per cent in both
1952 and 1956)—the religious issue hurt Kennedy more than it
helped him, in the final reckoning.[37] Kennedy's election, however, was largely attributable to the return of Catholics and
Southerners to the Democratic Party in key states, the keen
disaffection of Jews with Nixon and a resulting 81 per cent support for Kennedy, and at least a 70 per cent support from Ne-
groes. A substantial majority of Protestants were on the losing
side, arrayed against a coalition of minority religious and racial
groups and—statistically, the most important—a large minority
of white Protestants themselves. The foreign policy debates
staged the spectacle of a Catholic candidate preaching the mission of America with Calvinist zeal ("We must get America
moving again!") and a Protestant candidate increasingly assuming a defensive stance. That an Irish Catholic should sound
like a Puritan is not really strange: Roland Bainton once mused
that the Irish are not Catholic by nature and would have made
marvelous Protestants—for three centuries they have been *protesting* Catholics! Methodist Senator Karl Mundt blamed Nixon for
not showing the same evangelistic fervor which had won Republican campaigns in previous years. One Protestant writer hope-
fully regarded Inauguration Day 1961 as an occasion to "serve
symbolically as marking the end of Protestantism as a national
religion and its advent as the distinctive faith of a creative minority." The severing of this sentimental cord between Protestant piety and politics would involve a revitalizing realignment
of Protestant energies.[38]

Both the constituency of Congress and legislative voting
behavior in recent years tend to confirm the more general behavior of the electorate in religio-political matters. Congregation-

alists, Presbyterians, Episcopalians, and Unitarians have had about twice their share of representation. Methodists, Lutherans, and Baptists have been represented in approximate proportion to their membership. Catholics have been only about one-half to one-third represented, Jews one-third to one-sixth.[39] Sectional differences reflect the status of Protestantism: in the 85th Congress, 12 of 14 Protestant senators from the Northeast were Republican; in the Midwest, 16 of 18 were Republican; in the South, all 24 were Democrats. In the Northeast, 51 of 57 Protestant representatives were Republican; in the Midwest, 69 of 83; in the South, 98 of 106 Protestants were Democrats. Catholics and Jews, by contrast, were overwhelmingly Democratic—northern-style.[40]

There is a very practical lesson in such statistics: Protestant congressmen tend to be conservative and nationalist, with strongholds in the Republican Midwest and the Democratic South, while Protestant pronouncements tend to be liberal and internationalist. Ernest Best reported an interview with a congressman in which Best was speaking on behalf of Protestantism's official support for World Refugee Year: "I was silenced by the representative's claim that the greatest opposition to increased overseas aid and to increased immigration comes from those areas of the country where Protestant churches are strongest." [41] Thus does the "opinion gap" become a decisive factor in undermining the effective influence of elites in the denominations and in the National Council of Churches. Protestant lobbyists around Congress typically find more support for their pronouncements from Catholics and Jews than from fellow Protestants. Until this marginal character of Protestant leaders in their own constituencies is significantly changed, there will continue to be a fundamental fracture in Christian influence upon American policy. This fracture has been so wide in recent years that secular pressures have customarily prevailed without an effective challenge from the churches.

RELIGION
AS A SOURCE OF CONFLICT

TENSION BETWEEN CHURCH AND STATE

The fourth function of religion in world politics is to generate conflict between the religious community and the political community. That faithful religion may be the cause of political controversy is both a promise and a warning of the Scriptures: there is no guarantee of a peaceful co-existence between religion and politics. The Psalmist cried that the kings and rulers of the earth rejected not only the Lord but also His people.[1] The unhappy calling of Jeremiah, deeply loyal and patriotic as he was, set him in perpetual opposition to the elites of his time. Jesus foresaw an enduring conflict between his disciples and the decision-makers: ". . . and you will be dragged before governors and kings for my sake."[2] Such, indeed, was the Crucifixion itself.

The Cross is a political symbol before it is a religious one: it is a symbol of the inevitable tension between political loyalty and religious loyalty, between state and church. Christianity can never become completely domesticated within any nation: it is an inherently missionary fellowship with a certain foreign status within every secular community. Dietrich Bonhoeffer, whose martyrdom in Nazi Germany incarnated this tension so tragically and eloquently, declared that the very call of the Church to all men everywhere to join its fellowship in the Body of Christ

> is foreign to the world; the Church herself, in bearing this testimony, finds herself to be foreign to the world. Yet even

this is always only an ever-renewed consequence of that fellowship with the world which is given in the Body of Christ. The Church is divided from the world solely by the fact that she affirms in faith the reality of God's acceptance of man, a reality which is the property of the whole world.[3]

PROTESTANT MISSIONS AND POLITICAL TENSION

Tocqueville once observed: "If you converse with these missionaries of Christian civilization, you will be surprised to hear them speak so often of the goods of this world, and to meet a politician where you expected to find a priest." [4] While some missionaries have sought to deny the connection between religious and political influences which is inherent in the missionary vocation, historians and political scientists have repeatedly called attention to it. Perhaps no other aspect of religion's involvement in social forces has provoked greater controversy among students of religion. An historic vista is afforded by Kalijarvi:

> One reason why the West attained world political supremacy may be found in the restless, dynamic character of the Christian religion as it struggled for survival in ancient Rome, as it established its supremacy throughout Europe, as it fought for the recovery of the Holy Land during the Crusades, as it spread its missionaries everywhere. The Christian missionaries in the New World, Africa, Oceania, and the Far East have at once been agents of the church they represented and also powerful advance representatives of the states from which they came.[5]

Varg interprets the revitalized missionary movement at the turn of the century as "the religious counterpart of the new political forces that were stirring men's souls." Dwight L. Moody's revivals were essentially mission-oriented and launched the Student Volunteers for Foreign Missions with their ambitious slogan, 'The Evangelization of the World in this Generation." In no previous or subsequent period of American history did young people enlist so enthusiastically in a Christian crusade as they did in the generation before 1917. John R. Mott, Robert E. Speer, and Sherwood Eddy were "contemporaries of the busi-

nessman with an eye to foreign markets and of the new statesman with an irrepressible urge to cast the weight of American
influence onto the scales of international power politics." [6] The
period 1890-1917 was marked by the highest degree of missionary
fervor:

> Granted that a Christian sense of oughtness inspired the mis-
> sionary, it is also true that the missionary movement and im-
> perialism were wheels driven by the same explosive energy
> generated by a sense of superiority, moral duty, and the ego
> satisfaction to be gained in developing the underdeveloped
> areas of the world in the image of one's own society. The
> difference lay not so much in the nature of the generating
> forces which gave the impetus to the two movements but
> rather in their aims. American imperialism aimed at a goal
> circumscribed by a nationalistic faith in American institu-
> tions; the missionary movement in general accepted these
> goals but also, at its best, transcended them and envisioned a
> world brotherhood where human values would take prece-
> dence over national loyalties.[7]

Among the patterns of missionary influences upon foreign
policy are: (1) the direct participation of missionaries in the work
of the diplomatic corps; (2) the securing of special treaties and
other agreements protecting the status of missionaries; (3) the
stimulation of nationalism in mission countries, both positively
in the encouragement of nationalist aspirations and negatively
in the crystallization of mass hostility; (4) the sympathies and
hostilities generated by missionary education in American public
opinion; and (5) the direct pressure of missionary lobbies upon
policy-makers.

During the nineteenth century, missionaries performed important official and unofficial services for the American government in various countries. Among these were: Peter Parker
(1804-1888), medical missionary who served as legation secretary
and then commissioner in Peking in the 1850's; Samuel Wells
Williams (1812-1884), head of the Mission Press in Canton who
assisted Admiral Perry as an interpreter in Japan and served as
legation secretary in both China and Japan; William A. P. Martin (1826-1916), President and Professor of International Law at

Tung Wen College in Peking, first president of the Imperial University of China, and interpreter for the American legation in Peking; Arthur H. Smith (1845-1932), "influential" in determining China policy; Horace N. Allen (1853-1932), first Protestant missionary to Korea, who helped to establish the Korean legation in Washington and served as U. S. minister-resident in Seoul; and James L. Barton (1855-1936), foreign secretary of the mission Board in Turkey and "highly influential" in the conduct of United States policy in the Near East.[8] While it is difficult to measure just how influential these missionaries may have been in determining American policy, it is significant that such activity identified them with the interests of the American government in their mission work and in the thinking of the peoples to whom they were missionaries. Trade and access by missionaries were the two principal objectives of nineteenth-century diplomacy in the Far East. Neumann claims that the second of these objectives provided the characteristic shape of American diplomacy: "American policy was different from European because it was a missionary policy." In 1852, Congressman Chandler described that policy as "but an example of popular virtue, republican simplicity, and world-teaching example."[9]

Missions have been involved in diplomacy not only through personal services but also as the special objects of treaties of protection negotiated by the American government (frequently in concert with other Western powers) with Asian and African nations. Cushing's treaty of 1844 with China, which secured commercial privileges, extraterritoriality, and promises of protection for Christian missions, was negotiated with the assistance of Peter Parker and Samuel Wells Williams. According to Bailey, the consequences of this agreement were these:

> Missionaries from the United States, assured of a foothold under the Cushing treaty, came to China in increasing numbers, and extended their activities into the interior. These earnest soul savers, though a source of disturbance to the Chinese, were of some assistance in facilitating the work of diplomacy, and of great service in awakening American interest in the Celestial Empire. Throughout the forty years after 1847 books written by missionaries, though reflecting a

Christian bias, were the most reliable sources of information about the Far East generally circulated in the United States.[10]

While this account highlights the importance of the Cushing and subsequent treaties in protecting missions and in stimulating resentment abroad, it also illuminates the controversy between secular and church historians concerning religious influence. Students of foreign policy have been primarily exposed to the skepticism of diplomatic annals; churchmen have been inspired by the sagas of sacrifice narrated by the missionary historian. (Those who have read this study in various stages have offered conflicting advice as to the most relevant evidence. It seems useful, however, for supporters of missions to become familiar with the critical literature of secular scholars; a sample of that literature is offered in this chapter. The reconciling role of missions is discussed in chapter seven.)

A balanced view is that Protestant missions constitute an unexcelled chronicle of courage and devotion which too often has been slighted by the cynicism of critics; that the missionary enterprise remains an intrinsic and vital element in the work of the World Church; that American foreign policy and the United Nations have both profited greatly from missionary experience; that nonetheless missions have revealed the understandable limitations of denominational competition, national character, political education, and cultural awareness; and that missions cannot be totally divorced from political developments in which they have performed an important if largely unconscious role. Much of the criticism is based upon the unfortunate assumption of "guilt by association" with imperialism, militarism, and white supremacy.

That many Chinese were disturbed by the work of Christian missions seems true enough. The securing of special privileges for Christians, backed by the military might of foreign governments, provoked the most bitter reactions. Some mission stations unwittingly became legal sanctuaries for convicts who professed to be Christians, thus frustrating law-enforcement and court procedures. The mission-oriented policy of the American government in the nineteenth century helped to store up profound resentments within the soul of China—resentments which were not perceived by an American public unaware that the nation had any foreign policy. The race prejudice of a few missionaries aroused additional bitterness; paradoxically, the compassion and social justice which marked mission work with lower classes inflamed the hostility of privileged mandarins jealously defending the status quo. It goes without saying that the Christian minority in China gratefully attributed their conversion and new opportunities in education and health to missionaries from abroad. Dr. T. T. Lew, one of China's most prominent Christian leaders, testified in 1922 that "the great foundation of the Church has been laid by the devoted servants of God, both the missionaries and the Chinese Christian workers. The martyrs' blood which soaked the cornerstone is still fresh."

Martyrdom and militarism mixed tragically at the turn of the century. The "save-the-world-in-this-generation" zeal of the 1890's met an explosion of anti-Western animosity. When the Methodist Girls' School at Nanking was destroyed by a mob in May, 1891, Charles Denby, U. S. Minister in Peking, demanded punishment; the Chinese government arrested mob leaders and decapitated two of them. After the slaying of eleven missionaries in the village of Huashan in August, 1898, American denominational leaders called for justice; twenty-six Chinese were beheaded by their government. In March of 1900, as Secretary of State Hay was triumphantly announcing in Washington that the Open Door Policy had become "final and definitive," an aggressive band of Chinese revolutionists called Boxers launched a campaign of violence to expel "foreign devils." The Boxer Rebellion in North China killed 136 Protestant missionaries, 53 missionary children, 44 Catholics, and several thousand Chinese Christians. Cemeteries were desecrated. Foreign legations in Peking were besieged under a reign of terror which lasted for nine weeks; the German Minister and the Japanese Chancellor of Legation were murdered. Finally, the rebellion was crushed when an international expedition including American troops and commanded by a German general marched to Peking, plundered the capital, and remained to enforce the terms of the Protocol which was imposed

upon the Chinese government in 1901: an indemnity of $333,-
000,000 was exacted and Western powers were granted occupation rights in the legation quarter and at strategic points between
Peking and the sea. American diplomats were credited with exercising a moderating influence upon these demands.[11] A substantial portion of the indemnity was later returned to China
for educational purposes—and in recognition that the claim for
damages was excessive. Some missionaries refused to receive
compensation for their losses.

The Boxer Rebellion shocked both diplomats and missionaries. More than any other single event, it fractured the coalition
of missionary and political interests which the nineteenth century
had created. While some American consuls and other officials
had previously expressed irritation or cynical amusement at
missionary behavior, they had been unwilling to jeopardize their
careers by public criticism in a generation of evangelical fervor.
There had been resentment among diplomats when missionaries
helped to block the appointment of W. W. Rockhill as Minister
to China in 1897. When Theodore Roosevelt succeeded in winning approval for the appointment of Rockhill eight years later,
it was upon the latter's promise to "do his best to defend missionary interests." [12] Nevertheless, a growing uneasiness among
mission leaders over treaty provisions and the use of force to back
them followed the violence in which they were caught at the
beginning of a new century. With missionary support, a new
treaty was negotiated with China in 1903 which retained extraterritoriality but provided that Chinese Christians would be subject to the duties of citizenship and the jurisdiction of the courts.
They were, however, guaranteed religious liberty by the Chinese
government.

The coupling of Christianity with Western imperialism was
not generally perceived by American Protestants. An exception
was Methodist Bishop Francis J. McConnell who wrote in 1920
that

> as a matter of almost obvious historic truth, imperialism in
> the church is very apt to follow imperialism in commercial
> or political development. This is all the more probable be-

cause the tendency is so unconscious on the part of ecclesiastical leaders. Many of the most devoted churchmen may not be able to detect this parallelism between the national and the ecclesiastical movement even after it has been pointed out.[13]

But if Protestant America was slow to detect this connection and its international implications, a Communist government not yet three years in power in Russia canceled its unequal treaties with China in 1920. The Soviet Union was alert to the deeper meaning of the revolution in China and was able to free itself from the charge of imperialism while shifting the burden of that word to the capitalist nations of the West. Missionaries who had come to favor further treaty revision now found themselves, in fact, opposed by commercial interests which had acquired an increasing influence over American policy and which sought to maintain their special privileges.

As the Communist movement spread in North China in the 1920's, missionaries were exposed to new dangers. In Communist territory, a number of missionaries were driven out; some were killed; mission property was destroyed. There were increasing attacks by bandits which neither Communist authority nor Western power was willing to prevent by force. Western governments generally became reluctant to consider military action as a means of defending Christians in China; the effect of this reluctance was to increase the insecurity of missionaries and to encourage the anti-Christian movements (some of which were non-Communist) to still further violence. Paralleling the weakening of government protection was a sudden decline in home support for missions, both in financial backing and in general enthusiasm —a decline which was to continue into the Depression years. Church membership itself was falling off. These were the years of postwar disillusionment and craving for normalcy when it appeared that the Protestant zest for action had become a thing of the past. Yet thousands of missionaries remained in China through the 1930's and 1940's, and the churches continued to win Chinese converts. The heroism of many Americans who stayed after the Japanese invasion—some to be martyred for their identification with the Chinese cause—won a new respect for Christianity among its critics, both Western and Eastern. However, it was not until 1943, with Chinese-American co-operation at a premium in wartime alliance, that the United States finally surrendered its objectionable extraterritoriality—just 100 years after the original Cushing treaty.

Christian missions have also given a much more positive stimulus to nationalism abroad. This, notwithstanding a principle long affirmed by missions in theory but violated in the inevitable energies released by a dynamic international movement: "Missionaries should have nothing to do with political agitation. This is outside their sphere, and engaging in it can only harm their work." [14] However, the final report of the World Missionary Conference, which drafted that principle at Edinburgh in 1910, revealed intense concern over the dilemmas of many missionaries who were almost unavoidably finding themselves champions of the social and political aspirations of the people with whom they worked. Many offered to assist the governments of mission countries as advisers in matters of education, literacy, health, agriculture, handicraft industries, finance. Mission leaders had long experience in the management of such enterprises under church auspices.

This practical influence of Christian missions cannot be disentangled from the profound ideological impact of the missionary movement as the bearer of both radically different religious values and the political values of Western democracy. Chester Bowles records that, although they "promised not to engage in politics, their gospel of equality under God had profound political implications." [15] In nation after nation, the Christian missionary has stimulated a passion for freedom and has nurtured a native leadership in an ideology of progress and humanitarianism. Once again, we witness the gap between the intent and the effect of religious influence—between the manifest functions of religion and the latent functions.

Indian leaders have frequently testified to the revolutionary impact of Christianity. The leveling influence of mission teaching and practice stimulated the aspirations of lower castes while provoking a nationalist resentment from the defenders of the caste system. Gandhi's nonviolent approach to Indian independence was credited by him to Tolstoy and the New Testament as well as to the traditions of nonviolence in Hinduism. But Gandhi and other nationalists charged that the evangelistic methods of some missionaries used the educational and medical programs as inducements to baptism and church membership.[16] In the thirties, Hindu nationalists succeeded in securing discrimination against Indian Christians at some levels of government. Missionaries, as non-Indians, could not directly interfere in politics without provoking a hostile reaction—but their very non-participation was subject to the charge of cowardice or sympathy with British imperialism. In time, Indian Christians were drawn more and more into the independence movement: they felt obliged to prove themselves as persons who belonged to the Indian nation, even at the risk of antagonizing non-Christians still further. In India, as in China, some of the most zealous Christian intellectuals moved into the Communist camp, particularly a number of those who had experienced the frustration of being forbidden by church leaders to engage in political controversy.

Missionaries have thus acutely experienced the inescapable dilemma of religion-in-politics which Christian leadership encounters in every setting: *both intervention and non-intervention are causes of political conflict.*

After Indian independence was achieved, anti-Christian sentiment assumed new forms. The charge that missions were being manipulated as subversive outposts of American foreign policy has been made by Hindu zealots and, of course, by Communists. While India was established as a secular government along federal lines, some of the states (reminiscent of early American treatment of non-Protestants) have sought to impose special hardships upon Christians. The 1956 report of a six-member committee appointed by the government of the state of Madhya Pradesh declared:

> Evangelization in India appears to be a part of the uniform world policy to revive Christendom for reestablishing Western supremacy and is not prompted by spiritual motives. The

objective is apparently to create Christian minority pockets with a view to disrupting the solidarity of the non-Christian societies, and the mass conversion of a considerable section of *Adivasis* [aborigines] with the ulterior motive is fraught with danger to the security of the state. . . . The manner in which the missionary movement goes on in certain places is clearly intended to serve some political purpose in the cold war. . . . The best course for the Indian churches to follow is to establish a united independent Christian Church in India without being dependent on foreign support.[17]

This attack upon missionary motives is an obvious distortion; it is nonetheless an indication of the quality of political hostility which missions often confront in the new nations.

Diplomatic histories of the Middle East, Africa, and Latin America record this inevitable involvement of Christian missions in the dynamics of modern nationalism. For decades, the protection of missions was the most difficult problem of American diplomacy in the Middle East, where militant Christianity encountered militant Mohammedanism in such obstructions as: interference with the distribution of religious literature; interception of missionary mail; refusal to issue building permits for mission schools and churches; the denial of customs immunity for mission supplies which treaties had guaranteed; delays in prosecution of criminal acts against missionaries and their personal property. Diplomatic intercession by the United States government compounded the hostility. Apparently, such incidents were deliberately contrived at times by some nationalists who attacked mission property for the purpose of bringing about the hated foreign intervention. In the long run, the most far-reaching effect of Middle Eastern missionaries is to be found in the side effects of their activities. Although they were not politically minded, they were politically influential. "If the missions were seed beds of revolution, it was quite unintentional in the opinion of most writers."[18]

In 1885, the United States participated in the Conference of Berlin on African development which dealt especially with colonial competition and trade, but also provided for the protection of all religious institutions and Christian missionaries, scientists, and explorers. Thus were evangelism and economics linked in the exploitation of another continent. Coleman characterizes the historic role of missions in Africa as a "source of alternative values" furnishing "unintended consequences" for the continent's political life: it is "an established fact that those areas where the conversion has been greatest have showed the greatest nationalism." While some church leaders attempt to limit responsibility for this reaction to fundamentalists, even the Anglican and Catholic churches seem to have provided fertile sources of nationalist aspirations in Uganda and other countries.[19]

The problems of identification, both with African nationalism and with Western militarism, presented painful dilemmas to Protestant missions as the Congo obtained its independence from Belgium in 1960. At Coquilhatville, when United States Army planes landed, mobs of Congolese believed that the pilots had come to liberate them from the hated Belgian paratroopers. Lining the roadside, they smiled and waved, chanting in unison "Vive les Americains!" The pilots waved and smiled back. They could not anticipate the despair that followed when the Congolese learned why the pilots had come: to evacuate American missionaries. "But you came to help us," Congolese protested to a missionary. "We have to go," was the reply. "Our ambassador in Leopoldville says so." "Please, tell him to let you stay. Without you Americans we are lost." After Belgian evacuation from Matadi, fighter planes had returned in a "sneak attack, bombing and strafing the city at random." Enraged Congolese attacked the American Baptist mission, subduing its men and raping two women. It was then that United States Ambassador Clare Timberlake ordered all American missionaries to leave the Congo.[20] Most missionaries found it possible to return to the Congo in 1961, some to perform useful services for the new government and for the United Nations.

American Methodists were keenly troubled by the conflict between Moise Tshombe's Katanga Province and the United Nations-sponsored government in Leopoldville. Tshombe was educated in Methodist mission schools and became a prominent layman in the church. Both American and U.N. policy officially came to regard him as an erratic obstructionist and the chief obstacle to political progress in the Congo. On the other hand, Methodist Bishop Newell Booth and Methodist Senator James O. Eastland (Democrat from Mississippi) defended Tshombe's behavior as misunderstood and misinterpreted by the American public. Eastland's defense of Tshombe, through a Free Katanga Committee, was based upon the claim that the Katanga leader was the most forceful "Christian anti-Communist" in Africa.

Samuel Flagg Bemis, perhaps the most widely read of American diplomatic historians concerned with Latin America, has written that United States policy in that continent has had a moral and missionary background from the beginning. "Originally derived from Protestant Christianity . . . it has received a missionary impulse to save peoples not only from political tyranny, but also from political instability, from ignorance, from disease, from poverty."[21] Bemis credited the missionary endeavor with being the inspiration of the Good Neighbor Policy. More recently, both the Alliance for Progress and the Peace Corps have been ascribed by government leaders themselves to the missionary impulse of the American body politic.

In sum, it may be said that Protestant missions in Asia, Africa, and Latin America for more than a century have been identified with the activities and policies of the United States diplomatic corps and with the treaties which a number of nations came to associate with Western imperialism. More positively, Protestant missions, through the ideological impact of their teachings and institutions, have provided a major cause of the revolutionary ferment which American foreign policy has confronted upon those three continents since 1945.

PRESSURE GROUPS AND POLICY-MAKERS

Abraham Lincoln complained during the Civil War that he had been "approached with the most opposite opinions and advice, and that by religious men, who are equally certain that they represent the Divine will."[22] Policy-makers since Lincoln have had to bear the political consequences of religious tension within the American body politic: personal resentment, stalemate on some issues, manipulation of religious differences for political gain. In the United States, policy-making becomes especially difficult, if not impossible, when confronted by

> Catholic suspicion on one side, by Protestant suspicion on the other. A policy which, whatever its motives, may end in the destruction of the possibility of Catholic life in Poland, for instance, or the physical destruction of Rome, will be seen very differently by those who care for Catholicism and for Rome and by those who don't. The American Catholic . . . tends to make the attitude of a foreign government toward the Catholic church a touchstone of its decency, as Jews do treatment of Jews.[23]

And as Protestants do treatment of Protestants, it may be added. American diplomacy has at times confronted religious conflict at home which was not simply a sanction for diverse national origins but where religious interests themselves were primary factors. That is, religious conflict cannot simply be reduced to other forms of conflict—ethnic, class, sectional—but is a consequence of competing loyalties, traditions, and doctrines. There is a reciprocal influence between religious and political conflict: neither is wholly a function of the other.

When recognition was extended to the Carranza government of Mexico on the eve of World War I, there were pressures on President Wilson from various directions. Catholics complained that the disestablishment of their church by the new government was injurious to their religion and that American recognition seemed to sanction that action. At the same time, Wilson was accused of pro-Catholicism by outspoken Protestants, particularly because his private secretary, Joseph P. Tumulty, happened to be Catholic. Some imagined that Tumulty was a spy for the hierarchy and that the Pope was about to take control of the government in Washington. These conflicting pressures effectively neutralized each other and enabled Wilson to maintain recognition.[24] Later, Presidents Coolidge in 1926 and Roosevelt in 1934 were urged by Catholic leaders to intervene in Mexico. A diplomatic break was sought, the Mexican consulate was picketed, and there were Catholic boycotts of Mexican goods. But American policy was not to be reversed in the years of the "Good Neighbor."[25]

The Spanish Civil War excited intense religious controversy in the United States. According to Lubell, Catholic-Protestant polarization over that conflict remains (as of 1956) "one of the more important political dividers in the country. Both Catholics and non-Catholics still are fighting to vindicate the positions they took in that struggle."[26] American Catholics generally supported Franco, who had the unqualified backing of the Vatican, although some liberal Catholics exhibited their unhappiness with that position. While Catholic groups lobbied for the recognition of Franco, there was pronounced sympathy for the Republican government in liberal Protestant circles. American policy remained equivocal. When the United States blockade against supplies to Spain appeared on the verge of being lifted (which would have bolstered the Republican position), President Roosevelt at length declined to do so, allegedly because of pressure invoked during the visit of high church dignitaries (Catholic) to him concerning the matter.[27]

At times, religious groups have criticized the State Department for alleged discrimination in the selection or assignment of diplomatic personnel, as well as in the administration of such routine services as the issuance of passports. It was reported in the late thirties that the Department had adopted a policy of using only Roman Catholics as cultural attachés or consular officials in Latin American countries. As the hierarchies in those countries have stepped up their campaign against Protestant missions, there have been repeated claims by Protestants that they have had difficulty in securing passports. Both Christian and Jewish leaders have criticized American understandings with Saudi Arabia which provide that no Jewish personnel will be employed in official relationships with that country.

Periodically, the issue of diplomatic representation to the Vatican has been aired by American opinion. While the first of a number of consuls to the papacy was appointed in 1797, the declared opposition of such Protestants as James Madison to full political recognition of the Pope was the position which generally prevailed until 1848. In that year, after many Americans had responded favorably to the reform policies of Pius IX, President Polk appointed the U. S. legation secretary in Paris, Jacob L. Martin, as *chargé d'affaires* at Rome—though not without heated debate in the Senate. Various ministers followed Martin to that post until 1867, when restrictions on Protestant worship within Rome city limits aroused Protestant opinion and led to the closing of the mission.

The issue did not create a public clamor again until late 1939, when President Roosevelt sent holiday greetings to Pius XII, George Buttrick (then president of the Federal Council of Churches), and Cyrus Adler (prominent Jewish educator), proposing discussions of "our parallel endeavors for peace and the alleviation of suffering." Non-Catholics were not disturbed until it was learned that the President had decided to send Myron C. Taylor as his personal representative to the Pope. To many, this seemed like formal diplomatic procedure, and the general reaction elicited from the White House the explanation that Taylor's appointment was only temporary, that he would serve without salary and would not be formally accredited by the State Department. For a time, the Federal Council reluctantly accepted the appointment on that basis, although many Protestant leaders continued to speak and write in opposition to it. *The Christian Century* editorially regarded the whole affair

> not as a peace move but as a political move. Roman Catholics will be greatly pleased and can be counted on to remember it at the polls. Protestants and Jews are expected to be diverted by the sop in the invitations to Dr. Buttrick and Dr. Adler, and to forget it long before November. In that expectation we predict that the President will be disappointed.[28]

Just how many Protestants and Jews "remembered" in the election of 1940 is problematical in view of Roosevelt's generally strong support for a third term, which the *Century* opposed. However, pressure was again put upon the White House when President Truman declined to recall Taylor at the end of the war. When the personal representative finally retired in 1950,

Truman appointed General Mark Clark to succeed him. There was sufficiently effective protest by Protestants and Jews for Truman's position to become untenable, and Clark stepped aside. No subsequent appointment has been made.

The fact that religious groups seek to bring pressure to bear upon policy-making is not recognized by many members of those groups. There is a low degree of public awareness of the activities of denominational and ecumenical lobbies. Bone's study of American politics points to the relative invisibility of religious pressure groups:

> The separation of church and state and the popular assumption that politics and religion should not mix have obscured the fact from many Americans that there is a formidable "church lobby" both in Washington and in the states. In 1930 very few religious groups had an office in the nation's capital. Nowadays nearly every major denomination has a Washington representative.[29]

One of the reasons for this invisibility is that some of the largest denominations do not admit to themselves or anybody else that they are pressure groups or lobbies. Methodist agencies, recognized by policy-makers as exercising the influences appropriate to the nation's largest single denomination, have declined to register as lobbies, insisting that their work is educational. By contrast, some smaller groups frankly and openly acknowledge that their purpose is lobbying and register in compliance with the Federal Registration of Lobbying Act. Among such overt lobbies is the Friends Committee on National Legislation, whose general purpose is "to contribute effectively in the process of shaping important decisions by Congress and other agencies of the Federal Government on causes that Friends have at heart." The small circle of Friends and other pacifists is not visible to most American Protestants on foreign policy issues except as pacifist demonstrations win press headlines.

Another reason for the invisibility of Protestant pressure groups—and perhaps the most important—is the marginal status of both pronouncements on foreign policy and the denominational representatives who bring them to the attention of policy-makers. It is here that the "opinion gap" is perceived by political leaders even though religious leaders may pretend to speak for their constituencies. Politicians tend to be most responsive to the pressures of those groups which can command powerful rewards and punishments from their constituents: solidarity of opinion and support or opposition at the polls. "They are wise enough to know that a pronouncement by a Baptist convention will not be the opinion of all Baptists, that a statement by the National Council of Churches will not represent the thinking of all American Protestants, and that a position taken by the Commission of the Churches on International Affairs of the World Council will not have the considered support of world Protestantism. This by no means implies that public officials are indifferent to church opinion; it suggests rather that they take the opinions for what they are—those of a few leaders of better than average standing."[30]

Periodically, Protestant bodies have embarked upon short-term crusades to convert mass opinion into political influences. In 1924, Protestant missionary leaders launched a campaign against the militarism of the treaties which had guaranteed mission protection in China and other countries. Eighteen missionary societies and a majority of Protestant denominations agitated for treaty revision. The campaign caught the "old China hands" in the State Department unprepared politically. It now seemed to these career men with long memories that the inconsistency of Protestant fervor had come full-cycle: in former years, when on occasion they had not rigidly enforced the treaties, they had been subjected to outraged condemnation by missionary interests. While some Protestant leaders expressed repentance for the actions of previous generations, the zeal of the new campaign against militarism provoked an understandable resentment and skepticism. Arrayed against the forces of religion were those business interests which would be most threatened by the loss of extraterritoriality. The latter prevailed until the one effort for renegotiation was halted by the Japanese attack on Manchuria.[31]

The Manchurian Incident was the signal for a new campaign by Protestant leaders against the militarism and atrocities of the

Japanese who were contrasted with the "peace-loving Chinese" during the 1930's. In 1937, the renewal of aggression against China provoked more organized missionary publicity against Japan. John Leighton Stuart reports a 1937 conversation in China with Walter Judd, then a medical missionary, who had witnessed Japanese conquest in the Shansi region and was particularly disturbed by the fact of Japanese dependence on America for the basic materials of war. Judd declared that

> he must tell the American people of the iniquitous traffic which made us participants in these depredations. It meant leaving China for as long as the Japanese remained in power, resigning with no resources of his own from his Mission Board, starting on a crusade with no slightest assurance that the American public would care to listen to him or that even his minimum travel expenses could be provided. He had had some success in public speaking as a student, and that along with his burning conviction of having a burden on his soul of which he must deliver himself were his only assets. . . . As he related to me instances of Japanese cruelty and described the consequences to China if this were allowed to go unchecked, he became passionately excited. When he asked for my advice I could only urge him not to waste his energies on persons like me but to expend his fiery eloquence on the people at home. This he accomplished with marvelous success, and it opened the way for his continuing usefulness to China as a distinguished member of Congress. Fortunately for all concerned, a committee had already been formed for the very purpose he had in mind, and they were on the lookout for speakers when he arrived.[32]

The committee which had been organized was the American Committee for Non-Participation in Japanese Aggression, with headquarters in New York and with Henry L. Stimson as chairman and Harry B. Price as secretary. Protestant leaders urged their constituents not to buy anything made in Japan. Latourette has written of this campaign that "it was churches through their missionary education who had done most to familiarize Americans with the Far East and to create sympathy for China, the sufferer from the Japanese advance. Many Christians, by opposing the sale of scrap iron to Japan . . . contributed to the mount-

ing feeling against the Japanese programme and so to the outbreak of war between Japan and the United States." [33] Anxious
to offset the passion of their protests were missionaries in Japan
who felt that the picture of China was one-sided and who were
uneasy over the hostility to the United States which was steadily
building up in the Japanese public.[34] The "marvelous success"
of Judd and others was evident in a poll conducted by the American Institute of Public Opinion in February of 1940, nearly two
years before Pearl Harbor: 7 out of 10 favored prohibition of
shipment of military supplies and materials to Japan, and 37
out of 38 expressed sympathy with China in the Chinese-Japanese
conflict.[35]

If pre-1941 opinion concerning China was primarily the
product of missionary education, an observation of George Kennan is an indication of the critical reaction of some of the diplomatic historians:

> Unquestionably, our relations to the peoples of the Far East
> had been colored by a certain sentimentality toward the Chi-
> nese—a sentimentality as disrespectful to them and as unhelp-
> ful to the long-term interests of our relations as the feelings
> of blind petulance into which it now has a tendency to turn.
> In general, we expect too much from our Asian friends in the
> way of intimacy and mutual liking. There is something pa-
> tronizing in this attitude of ours.[36]

"Blind petulance" refers to the tendency to idealize the
Chiang government and to express unremitting hostility to the
Mao government. In late 1945, Walter Judd revisited China as
a congressman and as "Chiang's chief defender in the United
States." There were other Protestant missionaries, however, who
were sharply critical of Chiang, including the North China Mission of the American Board who reported that they were "ap-
palled by the gross corruption of the Kuomintang." During
Judd's visit, however, they complained that they were unable to
make their report to him because he was "tense and emotional"
and "did all the talking."[37] Judd returned to the United States
and, as Stuart wrote, was of continuing usefulness to China in
Congress. Judd in the House and William Knowland in the

Senate provided moral support for the China lobby and helped to guarantee the persistent refusal of the American government to recognize Communist China in the 1950's.

Stuart was the last American ambassador to China (1946-1952) before the triumph of the Communists. The son of Presbyterian missionaries, he had been a teacher of New Testament and a missionary educator in China himself. His memoirs provide an interesting account of the role of missions in American policy. While he numbered many friends among both Communist and Kuomintang leaders before assuming the ambassadorship in 1946, his service as an American diplomat found him subject to the frustrations and resentments of both. Stuart repeatedly acknowledged the corruption and disorganization which had prevailed under the Kuomintang, but the introduction to his book by Hu Shih (Chinese ambassador to Washington 1938-1942) testifies to the persistent alliance between Chiang Nationalists and some American Protestants on foreign policy issues. After comparing Dean Acheson's Letter of Transmissal of the China "White Paper" with Matthew 27:24 which narrates Pilate's washing of hands, Hu Shih wrote: "Because of the betrayal of China at Yalta, because of its withholding of effective aid to China at crucial times, and, above all, because of its great power and undisputed world leadership, the United States was not 'innocent of the blood' of fallen China." [38]

The heavy emotional investment of American Protestants in the missionary movement in China continues: no country presents a policy problem which divides Protestant leaders more sharply. Some returned missionaries impressed by China's difficulties under Chiang have been disposed to favor some kind of recognition of the Communist regime. They have been reinforced by pronouncements of the National Council of Churches and several denominations calling for the reconsideration of American Far East policy. Such statements have been quickly repudiated by other churchmen and by congressmen organized into the Committee of One Million and pushing unanimous joint resolutions through Congress in virtually every session. A vigorous protest against the moral fervor of some Protestant support for Nationalist China was made by Miller in 1951: Protestants, he complained, had been

> long ecstatic over Generalissimo Chiang Kai-Shek. There was no evaluation or even presentation of the politics of his regime, of his sources of support, of his program for China, of his attitude toward opposition groups and civil liberties. There was simply a steady stream of praise, rising sometimes to the level of a litany, for the Generalissimo and his wife. Why? Because they are "good Methodists." [39]

Not all Protestant campaigns for the arousing of mass opinion in foreign policy matters have been directly related to foreign missions. Others include: the crusade of the peace movements for arbitration treaties prior to World War I; the organized support for the disarmament conferences of the inter-war years; the program of the Federal Council of Churches' Commission on a Just and Durable Peace, under John Foster Dulles, to win popular support for the United Nations during World War II; the campaigns against Universal Military Training in the late 1940's; and repeated attempts to increase foreign economic and technical assistance and aid to refugees. In all of these efforts, Protestant groups have been joined by some Catholic and Jewish leaders and organizations.

The "realists" have characteristically expressed a deep-seated antipathy to all crusades, even to the point of launching a crusade against all crusades. With Fensterwald they observe that there are "certain built-in features about crusades in general" which have the effect of terminating their effectiveness after a short time. "Crusades work emotions up to a level far above that which can be permanently maintained." [40] But if crusades often are inherently incapable of fulfilling their own objectives, they may have unintended consequences for policy-makers whose "gravest general problem," according to Almond, is that of "the instability of mass moods, the cyclical fluctuations which stand in the way of political stability." [41] Protestant elites during the twentieth century have repeatedly given their constituencies the cues for those mass responses which have made responsible and consistent policy difficult and, at times, impossible. As profes-

sional emotionalists, Protestant leaders have plunged into foreign policy discussion with a fervor not to be expended upon
most other issues. The very nature of modern foreign policy,
especially in a nation where popular controls are fundamental,
encourages the enthusiastic participation of certain types of persons, according to C. B. Marshall:

> The sweep of its problems gives foreign policy a special at-
> traction for those . . . born with a passion to reform the world.
> Foreign policy appeals to those inspired by identification with
> large and high-sounding public causes. Its complexities and
> subtleties are rich with opportunity for generalizers and ob-
> fuscators.[42]

From the perspective of policy-makers, more important than
the simple fact of participation by religious leaders is the quality
of that participation and, above all, whether it is sustained or
erratic participation.

The fact that policy-makers and diplomatic historians express
a large measure of cynicism concerning religious pressure groups
may not always reflect objective judgment. The most responsible
and intelligent religious action in the political arena will generate conflict. When that action does not support the positions
for which public officials are seeking to win approval, religious
leaders are exposed to the hazards which are confronted by all
pressure groups: "loss of influence when wrong, demoralization
when defeated, and the enmity of others."[43] These hazards beget
new and more subtle dangers: the temptations to martyrdom and
self-righteousness which serve inevitably to alienate religious
leaders from public officials and competing pressure groups.

Whatever the power of church lobbies may be, the transcendent and supranational claims of Christianity compel the
church to be a pressure group against the idolatrous claims of
the state. For Christians, as Morray suggests, there is a continuing "crisis of patriotism" or a "schizophrenia" of loyalties.[44]
Yinger makes the category of conflict explicit in his discussion
of the relationship between universalist religions and the nation
state:

> A universalist religion, consistently carried through, *mus*

conflict at various points with the political activity of a society, with its concern for only a segment of mankind and its ultimate appeal to force. . . . Unless the religious system around which the institutions have been built is completely destroyed, an implicit conflict will remain. Despite the enormous pressures toward the nationalization of religion in the modern world, it seems highly unlikely . . . that the universalist element in the world religions will ever be lost, however much those religions may change in theology, ritual, or organization.[45]

The very power of Protestantism to influence foreign policy is dependent upon its capacity to generate conflict. Unless it is able to establish and maintain loyalties which can challenge the power-structure of the state, Protestantism is reduced to the priestly function of blessing whatever government asks it to bless.

INTERNAL TENSIONS OF POLICY-MAKERS

The problem of church and state is not solely an institutional matter concerned with the relationship of vast hierarchical organizations. It is a problem which ultimately concerns individual human beings who must somehow accommodate both the religious and the political dimensions of their own experience. The vast majority of American policy-makers— Presidents, diplomats, congressmen—are not just political animals: they are also participants in the life of various religious communities themselves. Many are unquestionably sincere and devout in their professions of faith; a few may not be. The sensitive religious person employed by the government experiences the rival pressures of church and state with special force. When preachers, lay or professional, do not perceive these tensions within the soul of the policy-maker and simply call down moral judgments upon his head, they unwittingly alienate the policy-maker from the more positive graces of religious influence. When religious elites ignore the mix of ethical and technical dilemmas involved in decision-making, they become irresponsible leaders of public opinion. "The clergy, as much as any sector of the American public, need to be warned against underestimating the immensity of the problems faced by the government in making foreign policy and against the temptation to offer ready, often ill-considered solutions." [46]

Internal conflicts for policy-makers are not simply those of conflicting roles—churchman vs. politician—but rather are inherent in the very nature of policy-making in which values must be made relevant to concrete proposals for government action. It is at this point that the "realists" have concentrated their discussion of the relationship between the ultimate claims of Christian ethics and the relative claims of foreign policy. Niebuhr, Morgenthau, Lippmann, Kennan, Halle, Marshall, Bennett, Butterfield, and others have continuously portrayed the dilemmas of decision-making in all their tension, ambiguity, paradox, and compromise.

In 1943, Lippmann wrote that "in foreign relations, as in all other relations, a policy has been formed only when commitments and power have been brought into balance." [47] Decision-makers must not become so preoccupied with the ends of policy that they neglect the means necessary to the implementation of policy. Marshall's version in 1954 was that

> the goal aspect of foreign policy is essential. It is also easy. It is the easiest part of the business. The difficult part comes not in figuring out what one would do if one could do everything one may wish to do. It comes in deciding what to do in the circumstances of being able to do only part of what one may wish to do. That is the task of handling dilemmas and of rationing means. Here the making of foreign policy reaches the vital level. Here success is courted. Here failure is risked. [48]

Perhaps the most systematic statement of the internal conflicts built into the problems confronting policy-makers is that provided by John Bennett's discussion of the distance between Christian ethics and social policy. In addition to the experience of jealousy and hostility among decision-makers, Bennett lists: (1) the history of accumulated disorders, prejudices, vested interests, and vicious circles of fear, hate, and vindictiveness which sets the stage for all present decisions; (2) the fact that public decisions involve pluralistic communities in which only a minority may be Christians; (3) the impersonal relationships characteristic of large-scale problems; (4) conflicting group interests which intensify moral blindness; (5) the tendency to cloak self-interest with idealism; and (6) the dilution of personal responsibility among decision-makers. Beyond all these are such morally neutral factors as technical issues, the need for prediction, and the problem of choice among competing values.[49]

The religiously sensitive person cannot help experiencing these conflicts in acute form: his absolute religious loyalty must find expression in the relativities of political choice, but his sense of vocation is a response to the near-absolute claims of the nation-state upon him. These conflicts are not simply intellectual: they touch the deepest springs of personal feeling. It is in the individual that tensions between religious and political loyalties become an existential reality. Policy-makers with fundamental religious commitments continue to bear these conflicts only at great physical and psychological cost. They may respond to inner personal conflict by repressing it, compartmentalizing their loyalties, rationalizing their accommodation, unloading their tension upon others—or by deepening their religious insight into the meaning of the conflict, releasing the tension in ever-renewed dedication to their calling, absorbing the hostility of others without returning it, sharing the meaning of their religious loyalty with others. The Christian in politics, wrote Jerry Voorhis, "will constantly be confronted with the problem of half a loaf or none, and he will spend many a wakeful night wondering whether it is more nearly right to vote for the half loaf than to stand on principle and run the risk of getting none of it."[50] Democratic government, even at its very best, is "a process of compromise and reconciliation of the various opinions of many different people. And therefore the difficult and usually unsatisfying task of the individual representative is to work unceasingly and wisely for the absolute right in which he believes but to make his choices and decisions from day to day not between white and black but between light and dark shades of gray."[51]

Those entrusted with primary responsibilities as decision-makers in foreign policy bear potentially the most severe internal conflicts with which modern men can be burdened. It is in their decisions that the ultimately religious problems of mass death, frustration, and hostility must be confronted more directly and more constantly than in the making of any other kind of decision. It has been argued that the American President, with his final responsibility for foreign policy, should not be a strong Christian because of the awful tension which faith generates; that the strong Presidents have invariably been weak Christians.[52] It is only when one capitulates to the most narrow, moralistic carica-ture of a Christian that this argument is acceptable to the faith-ful Christian. "Realists," observing that "idealists" have often re-laxed the tension between ends and means in favor of the ends, have just as often relaxed that tension in favor of the means. Whatever the visible religious qualities of an American President and other policy-makers, their most difficult tasks require an ability to sustain the profoundest internal conflicts and to use them constructively.

Woodrow Wilson did not respond to international violence with the unambiguous enthusiasm of a simple idealist. Both the fidelity and the anguish of his Puritan conscience were revealed in the decision to enter World War I and in his personal cam-paign for the League of Nations. With regard to the former, Frank I. Cobb of the New York *World* provided the following account of a visit with Wilson in early April, 1917:

> I'd never seen him so worn down. He looked as if he hadn't slept, and he said he hadn't. He said he was probably going be-fore Congress the next day to ask a declaration of war, and he'd never been so uncertain about anything in his life as about that decision. For nights, he said, he'd been lying awake going over the whole situation. . . . "I think I know what war means," he said, and he added that if there were any possibil-ity of avoiding war he wanted to try it. "What else can I do?" he asked. "Is there anything else I can do?" [53]

RELIGION
AS A SANCTUARY FROM CONFLICT

The fifth function of religion in world politics is to serve as a sanctuary from political conflict. The Scriptures contain the vision of the Lord's holy mountain "where they shall not hurt nor destroy," [1] of a "shelter of the Most High" where his angels will guard the faithful,[2] of a personal ministry even to enemies where no vengeance can intervene.[3] The *koinonia*, the loving community, lifts itself above all hostilities to minister to both the participants in and the victims of violence. The community of faith is a fellowship of peril and hope which always, as John Bennett puts it, affords its members "a home, where in perplexity or under pressure from hostile forces they may find both light and healing."[4] Faithful Christianity must always transcend political struggles even while identifying deeply and relevantly with them.

The costs of international violence are ultimately personal. While the consequences of war may be measured in terms of property losses, changed boundaries, and altered governments, all of these acquire meaning only in relation to the experiences of persons: victory and defeat, pain and death, loneliness, family disruption, moral confusion, mental illness, mobility, hunger, disillusionment, hate, fear, heroism, cowardice, guilt. Whatever may be the ethical view for the justification of war, churches find their own most distinctive functions projected into the very circumstances of violence to minister to persons. Millions of Americans, indifferent to religious obligations in peacetime, turn to the guidance, the security, and the consolation afforded by the churches in time of war or threat of war. Worship and prayer do not become less evident in war, but more so; pastoral counseling is not less demanding in war—it is never subject to greater demand or greater need. The military chaplaincy, relief and refugee assistance, the wartime religious underground are all personal ministries in the midst of conflict. These activities bring religious leaders into working contact with government officials; such contacts may encourage both mutual appreciation and new church-state tensions.

The transcendent claim of faith provides the religious community with a certain orientation away from the purely political and military activity of states. As this function of sanctuary tends to dominate an ethical viewpoint absolutely, some persons will reject military and political claims against them. Some will refuse to bear arms or to pay taxes. Some will find religious sanctions for isolationism. Some will find any participation in politics an intolerable compromise—or they will seek to compartmentalize between the tensions of politics and "the spiritual life." They will quote Edmund Burke:

> Politics and the pulpit are terms that have little agreement. No sound ought to be heard in the church but the healing voice of Christian charity. . . . Surely the church is a place where one day's truce ought to be allowed to the dissensions and animosities of mankind.[5]

As the organic bonds between religion and politics are broken, new tensions are created: the very act of withdrawing from conflict may generate further conflict. The Puritan ambivalence in American politics has driven some citizens into the political arena with a peculiar moral fervor; it has also withdrawn citizens from that arena with a chronic moral disdain.

PACIFISM: REJECTION OF VIOLENCE

Just as there has been a persistent current of pacifism in Christianity since New Testament times, so there has been a continuing procession of peace movements throughout American history. As the United States became a world power at the turn of the century, peace societies experienced a spurt of growth and came to represent the prevailing mood of the churches. On Peace Sunday in 1909, 50,000 sermons on peace were preached in American pulpits. A common theme held that international violence was a thing of the past. The peace movement seemed to reach its fulfillment in 1912: Woodrow Wilson was elected President and pacifist William Jennings Bryan was appointed Secretary of State.[6]

In the conversion of American moral enthusiasm from peace to war in 1917, committed pacifists suddenly found themselves a persecuted minority. Protestant leaders were typically less willing than the War Department to seek the protection of conscientious objectors under law. Chaplains and Y.M.C.A. workers seemed especially determined to repudiate any fellow churchmen who remained opposed to the war. The American Unitarian Association refused funds to churches whose ministers remained pacifist. Methodist Bishop T. S. Henderson of Detroit made a pledge to regenerate or eliminate any antiwar pastors in his area. While perhaps as many as several hundred ministers retained various shades of pacifist conviction, those who were outspoken lost many members from their churches. Only the Fellowship of Reconciliation and the People's Council conspicuously continued to oppose the war, attempting to protect C.O.'s and to secure a definition of war aims—but even they lost some of their most prominent leaders. Many were sent to Federal prisons for their pacifist objections.

After the Armistice and the postwar disillusionment, there was a restoration of pacifism in Protestantism. Hundreds of ministers renounced their 1917 positions and returned to the peace movement. All major denominations passed resolutions opposed to war. By 1934, perhaps the high-water mark of pacifist power in American history, a survey of Protestant and Jewish clergy disclosed that 62 per cent would not sanction or participate in war and 67 per cent believed that the churches should refuse to sanction or support any war. Peace organizations flourished again. They exerted heavy pressures in support of disarmament conferences and urged the establishment of a Peace Department in the Federal government.[7]

It must be remarked, however, that pacifism's definition is variable, depending upon circumstances and upon individual interpretations. There are psychic factors shaping the size and strength of pacifism, including compulsions and aversions with regard to force generally. As Kennan has written:

> Force, like peace, is not an abstraction; it cannot be understood or dealt with as a concept outside of the given framework of purpose and method. If this were better understood, there could be neither the sweeping moral rejection of international violence which bedevils so many Americans in times of peace nor the helpless abandonment to its compulsions and its inner momentum which characterizes so many of us in times of war.[8]

The drives which carry moralistic fervor can lend a psychological consistency to a pacifist crusade and a military crusade. Militant pacifism, determined to resolve world tensions, creates political tensions of its own. In wartime, the pressures for conformity in loyal support of the war are so great that only a few seem willing to pay the social price and the personal costs of being categorized as pacifist. In peacetime, on the other hand, protesting against war can be "almost a hobby or fad, and can even win a degree of popularity."[9] Between the two world wars, pacifism's circle seemed to expand so wide as to include isolationists and intolerant fringe groups. Most persons more strictly defined as pacifist after 1918 were ardently internationalist (although some did refuse support to Wilson's campaign for the League of Nations because of his compromises at Versailles and the Covenant's provisions for collective security). It was, therefore, ironic that they should appear to some to be allied with pro-Nazi, anti-Semitic groups in pressing for nonintervention in the late thirties. Pacifism continued to have these associations in the public mind after 1941—a major factor operating to limit the strength of pacifism in subsequent years. The general support of the war effort after Pearl Harbor, while less enthusiastic than in 1917, demonstrates the minority status to which pacifism has been consigned in the almost unrelieved international conflicts of the two subsequent decades:

> Once again the churches exhibited how thoroughly inter-twined with the rest of society they are. The dilemma that they face is made manifest by the inevitable retreat of the great majority from a position of pacifism. Once more they have had to accommodate to an "inevitable," even though it may be far removed from their ethic. Even were their loyalties en-tirely religious, many thought that to stand aloof from the con-flict was not to stop it, but only to lose much of the influence for good that the churches might have had in the midst of it.[10]

Traditional pacifist sects, not without some dissension, generally refused to go along with the war. Pacifists in the major denomi-nations remained stronger than they had in 1917-1918, and many sought to mitigate hate and atrocity stories, defend civil liberties, improve race relations, and focus attention upon war aims and postwar planning. There was also more tolerance of conscientious objectors by the Federal law and by public opinion: this time the churches worked with the National Service Board for Religious Objectors in maintaining Civilian Public Service Camps. Prot-estantism more openly accepted its pacifist-non-pacifists differ-ences; both groups worked together in the interests of a "just and durable peace." Thus, pacifists were less extreme in their with-drawal from the conflict, and non-pacifists tended to be more re-strained in military fervor.

The atomic attacks upon Hiroshima and Nagasaki compli-cated the ethical discussion of violence after World War II; the development of hydrogen bombs and long-range missiles raised still other issues. By the late 1950's, the limited war debate and the National Committee for a Sane Nuclear Policy rallied many Protestants to new alternatives between the extremes of pacifism and unrestricted militarism. Accordingly, by 1960 seven groups could be identified within Protestantism along a continuum be-tween pacifism and militarism: (1) "absolute pacifists" opposed to force as an instrument of foreign policy or international or-ganization; (2) "police-force pacifists" willing to support force only under international controls through the United Nations; (3) "nuclear pacifists" opposed to nuclear weapons testing and stockpiling but willing to support the use of conventional weapons; (4) "just war theorists" appealing to the traditional Catholic principle of "non-combatant immunity" as a relevant restraint upon mass annihilation; (5) "limited war theorists" who would retain nuclear weapons as a deterrent but who want a flexible response capability based upon a range of nuclear and conventional weapons; (6) "massive retaliationists" who would base both diplomatic and military strategy upon nuclear weapons; and (7) "preventive war advocates" who would attack the Soviet Union in a forestalling blow while the United States retains an edge in destructive power. The continuing weakness of pacifism and the proliferation of ethical alternatives left Protestantism without a clear witness on military issues in the early 1960's. However, the Kennedy administration edged away from Dulles' massive retaliation doctrine and gave a renewed emphasis to conventional weapons, welcoming a number of limited war theorists into high policy councils.

ISOLATIONISM: REJECTION OF FOREIGN POLICY

> One may arrive at an isolationist position along more than one avenue. The nationalist rejects the limitations on power and discretion which alliances with foreign powers or participation in international organization implies. The utopian internationalist rejects the partialism of security diplomacy and the sordidness of political and economic means. He worships in the pure church of humanity redeemed. In effect, but not in intent, he often finds himself lodged in the same isolationist pew with the nationalist.[11]

That ardent nationalists felt they worshipped in the one true church was evident in the rhetoric of many religious and political leaders after 1918. Senator William Borah opposed American entrance into the League of Nations because he feared the contamination of pure democracy through official contacts with the imperialistic nations of Europe. He preached that the mission of America was to demonstrate democracy to the world;

democracy was more than a form of government: "It is a moral entity, a spiritual force as well. And these are things which live only and alone in the atmosphere of liberty." [12]

The outlawing of war through the Kellogg-Briand Pact of 1928 was a notable instance of pacifist-nationalist-internationalist collaboration in support of a policy regarded by its critics as isolationist because it lacked effective implementation. The United States did not thereby join the League of Nations nor did it assume any new obligations within an alliance. Hill and Lund characterize the Kellogg Pact as a church venture which began in 1923 and which was principally sustained by the Federal Council of Churches and *The Christian Century*. This characterization, made in criticism, was matched by the positive claim of Charles Clayton Morrison's *Century* editorial of January 24, 1929: "It was the readers of the *Christian Century* who made the outlawry of war a reality." [13]

In subsequent years, both diplomats and historians came to express intense scorn for the Kellogg Pact and its moral consequences. In Foster Rhea Dulles' estimation, it has become "almost universally agreed that the Kellogg-Briand Treaty had exercised a harmful rather than a helpful influence on the cause of world peace. The outlawry of war served to satisfy the conscience of the American people without requiring of them any positive action, and also created an illusion of safety which seemed to obviate the need for any more direct participation in world affairs." [14] The churches had generated a moral fervor which became a substitute for foreign policy and a distracting influence from the responsibilities of policy-makers. That the campaign for the treaty had been prompted by a profound passion for peace is unquestionable—the consequences were that Protestantism had bolstered isolationism and the prospects for aggression and war.

The Kellogg-Briand Treaty was repeatedly appealed to by both government and religious leaders in the 1930's. When the Japanese attacked Manchuria in 1931, Secretary of State Henry L. Stimson protested on moral grounds under the treaty. In time, Stimson came to favor active co-operation with the League of Nations and the imposition of economic sanctions against Japan.

He was, however, opposed by President Hoover who insisted that the treaty was not a military alliance but was enforceable solely by "the moral reprobation of the world." [15] In this internal conflict within the administration, many Protestant leaders swung to the support of the Stimson Doctrine as their stake in missions in North China and Manchuria asserted itself. Hoover, in addition to appealing to the moral arguments which the churches themselves had previously advanced, replied that he did not wish to aid the build-up of the military clique in Japan through external pressure.[16]

A Senate committee headed by Gerald P. Nye reported in late 1934 that United States and foreign munitions-makers had been "linked together to increase the sale of their products by bribery, lobbying, and other methods." Some Protestants responded to the revelations of the Nye Committee with an emotional simplicity which reduced the causes of war to one: profiteering by munitions-makers. The Federal Council and *The Christian Century* gave vociferous support to Senate hearings. One of the immediate consequences of the hearings was an effort to rally American opinion behind the Neutrality legislation introduced in 1935. A pronouncement of the Federal Council declared that the United States should withhold aid from all belligerents in any conflict that might arise. *The Christian Century* insisted that any nation "has a right to stay neutral at whatever cost, and that no cost which protects peace is too high." [17]

After the Neutrality Act was passed, military adventures multiplied in widely separated territories. Italy attacked Ethiopia in October, 1935; Germany sent troops into the demilitarized Rhineland in March, 1936; Germany and Italy both came to the support of Franco in the Spanish Civil War; Japan attacked China in the summer of 1937. While some Protestants were beginning to question the neutrality policy, isolationists and pacifists became more zealous in its defense. The latter groups expressed great alarm after President Roosevelt's "quarantine" speech of October 5, 1937, in which he referred to the epidemic of aggression in the world community. *The Christian Century's* reply to Roosevelt was notably hostile: "His attitude toward the neutrality law, his use of the 'quarantine' metaphor, his inveterate navalism, his need of distracting attention from certain unhappy features of his domestic policy and of rallying Congress to his support, his possible ambition to outdo the other Roosevelt with the latter's Treaty of Portsmouth, and the contingency of a possible third term ambition—these considerations work together in the public mind to cause and in considerable measure to justify much of the apprehension which exists." [18] Roosevelt himself later acknowledged that his speech had fallen "upon deaf ears—even hostile and resentful ears." [19]

Isolationism continued to receive some fervent Protestant sanctions until Pearl Harbor. In the 1950's, a neo-isolationism associated with elder statesman Hoover's "fortress America" concept, aroused some support from right-wing evangelists and politicians.

PRIVATIZATION: REJECTION OF POLITICS

Tocqueville observed a certain contempt for politics on the part of Protestant leaders in America: "And when I came to inquire into the prevailing spirit of the clergy, I found . . . that they made it the pride of their profession to abstain from politics." [20] This abandonment of the political arena to more worldly men has been characteristic not only of clergy but of "good people" generally in the Protestant churches. The Puritan's zest for reform has been matched by his fear of contamination. This moral repudiation of politics has been shared, strangely enough, by many Protestant leaders passionately concerned about peace as the primary goal of foreign policy. There has been a preoccupation with the United Nations and with international law and a corresponding neglect of the national policy-making complex: the President and executive departments, Congress, political parties, pressure groups. Of this anti-political approach to peace, Wriston has written:

> Diplomacy moves in the medium of politics; there is no other atmosphere available, and it is folly to seek one. Schemes for the elimination of political forces in diplomacy are simply ef-

forts to evade the facts of life. It is absurd to find men arguing for such a utopian program while pretending to deal realistically with world problems.[21]

The Puritan ethos has generated a "privatization" of life: a tendency to withdraw into a world of personal virtue and individual satisfactions. This not only means "letting George do it" in politics: it means a distorted interpretation of political life. In particular, it reinforces a pattern of "personality politics" in which such individual virtues as sincerity, honesty, thrift, and church membership are made to seem more important than the ability to make national policy serve realistic political goals.

But underneath these tendencies toward "privatization" have been running the swift counter-currents of "politicization"; the tendency of government to become more complex and more comprehensive in its impact on all of human life. There is a centrifugal process by which personal interests have been flung out to wider and wider circles of decision-making—local, state, national, international—and which has hurtled the individual American into the seemingly remote arena of world politics, whether he knows it or not. It becomes increasingly difficult for the citizen to give his attention to all the levels of policy which invade his own interests even if he is intelligent enough to be aware that the invasion is taking place.[22] The complexity and changes in government machinery, the demand for some understanding of such sophisticated matters as missile technology and international economics, the shifting pressures of invisible government (lobbies) behind the activities of legislation and diplomacy— these can overwhelm the citizen with a sense of his own powerlessness. "But what can one person do?" is the most familiar refrain in the ears of both preachers and politicians.

At the very time when a fateful premium is placed upon the American citizen's political understanding and skills, he may become most desperately preoccupied with his own private world —family, job, personal religion. The Protestant revival of the 1950's all too often pandered to these escapist tendencies: there was a notable resurgence of Puritan moralism which readily identified with a President, Eisenhower, who joined a church for the first time in his life and who spoke scornfully of politics and politicians. There is, at times, a vicious circle in the Puritan ethos in which public responsibility is underminded by the excesses of an anxious, piously conforming self-righteousness. This vicious circle is, in part, the product of those religious and political leaders who play upon the threat to survival without relating individuals to realistic action in the face of the threat. The American body politic, burdened with the global responsibilities of a great power as never before, is lacking in much of the ethical and political equipment required by those responsibilities. As William Lee Miller has put it: "This is what has happened: *a nation with a most unpolitical tradition has now become the nation that most urgently needs political understanding.*" [23]

Political alienation is the term which best describes this estrangement between personal life and public responsibility. This estrangement from politics is accompanied by the notion that insiders with influence make all government policy: "they" and not "we." That Protestants should experience a high degree of political alienation is not simply a direct consequence of the psychic properties of Puritanism: their political orientation is also a product of social mobility. White, middle class Protestants have been moving from cities to suburbs at a rapid rate for the past decade. Such mobility tends to destroy that local identification which is almost the first maxim of political success and the source of the highest degree of political interest. If Protestants still comprise a numerical majority in the United States, that statistical fact must be measured against two others: (a) the United States is an urban nation, and (b) urban centers are increasingly populated by non-Protestant and non-white groups. In part, the Protestant withdrawal from politics is a function of the Protestant withdrawal from the city. That withdrawal reinforces the Puritan image of city politics as corrupt, machine-ridden, and Catholic-controlled.

The alienation of surburban Protestants combines with the defensiveness of rural Protestantism to stalemate national policy in many critical fields. Both the political ideology of the American people and the ethical ideology of Protestantism—in reality,

one and the same thing—remain steeped in rural fundamentalism. The heritage of revivalism in rural Protestantism is scarcely
concealed in the fervor of political crusades which recur periodically—lately on the "radical right." Curiously enough, these crusades help to entrench the political status quo and not to transform it: rural domination of Congress, of state legislatures, of
both parties, and one-party rule in the Democratic South as well
as in the vast Republican domains in the North and Midwest.
Thus rural ideology combines with a shrewd exploitation of
the structures of American government. Moralism becomes a
mask for professional cynicism and self-serving interests.

For the political aliens of suburbia, Protestant influence upon
national policy has these liabilities: (1) the escape from the invasion of racial and religious minorities removes Protestant leadership from the stage of those domestic conflicts for which there
is now a worldwide audience, while actually intensifying those
conflicts within American society; (2) the abandoning of urban
centers weakens Protestant identification with those unsolved
economic and welfare problems which threaten the country with
domestic stagnation; (3) Protestants become more vulnerable to
the artificial compartmentalization between domestic and international issues, leaving them increasingly with the paradoxical
combination of a sentimental internationalism and a socioeco-
nomic conservatism; (4) the retreat from the city is a retreat
from exposure to the cosmopolitan and intercultural influences
of the city; and (5) Protestant participation is increasingly withdrawn from such national and international centers of foreign
policy discussion as New York, Boston, Baltimore, and Chicago.

The political alienation of Protestantism is perhaps finally
to be characterized as political immaturity. A free and responsible society requires enormous quantities of political maturity.
Within the context of a theory of conflict, political maturity for
contemporary Americans means facing up to those conflicts
which they would like to escape: urban-rural conflict, race conflict, interfaith conflict, economic conflict, partisan conflict. Each
of these conflicts, in turn, holds a special key to the ultimate

problem of international conflict. Political maturity, according to Levin, is

> the ability of an individual to handle feelings of political alienation through rational rather than regressive mechanisms. To achieve this, one must perceive the realities of the political structure, hold political goals which are potentially operational, and attempt to develop institutions through which these goals may be realized. Political maturity, like political alienation, refers to a quality of an individual rather than a system.[24]

American Protestantism has been plagued with a chronic aversion to controversy in politics. There is, however, no other kind of politics available—at least, not within a country whose proudest political institutions were designed to foster controversy and to prevent a monopoly of power or of ideas. There is, moreover, something within Christianity itself which seems to deny the fullest fruits of faith until that faith has been plunged into the middle of human tensions. This positive appreciation of the role of conflict has been well expressed by a Congregational pastor in Providence:

> Controversy in a church may be a sign that that church is on the frontier of real and urgent quests, beyond the periphery of the trite and over-simple where it comes face to face with the problems of human understanding and holds all slogans suspect. Controversy may be an indication of a venture into the realm of the ambiguous where we may come also to a comprehension of God's venture into the same world in Jesus Christ. Controversy may indicate involvement in irreconcilables where the only answer is self-sacrifice and the cross becomes more than a symbol. Controversy over vital issues may indicate alertness to real problems that defy solution, making necessary a supplication for the guidance of the Holy Spirit.[25]

In such a church, the sanctuary affords not only a shelter which transcends conflict but also the courage which identifies with conflict to wrest from it the highest ethical and spiritual achievements of which men are capable.

RELIGION
AS A RECONCILER OF CONFLICT

AMBASSADORS FOR CHRIST

The sixth and final function of religion in world politics is to reconcile political conflict. The Scriptures are a special anthology of dreams of reconciliation. Isaiah foretold the coming of a Prince of Peace whose universal government would be unending.[1] Micah prophesied the remolding of the tools of death into tools for the cultivation of fields and fruits.[2] The *koinonia,* the community of the New Covenant, expressed its ultimate loyalty to a Power whose very nature is to reunite those who have been separated by conflict: this is "the ministry of reconciliation" making us "ambassadors for Christ, God making his appeal through us." [3] There is a divine diplomacy working through the faithful and loving community.

But the ministry of reconciliation cannot be reduced to a single, simple category like unity or peace. The most relevant expression of Christian loyalty in its fullness depends upon the degree to which it recognizes, performs, and balances all of the other functions inherent in its dialectical relationship to the political community: identification with the political community in both peace and war, transcendence of the political community as a missionary fellowship which cannot be contained within political boundaries and which ministers to persons in the range of their human need. Peacemaking may be more than a political function—but it is not nonpolitical or anti-political. Yet Christianity must be the source of a continuing creative conflict be-

tween itself and the political community if it would exercise its
unique powers to resolve conflicts between political communities.
This is the concealed wisdom in the separation of church and
state. Bonhoeffer conceived of the twin loyalties to church and
state as divine mandates which are finally to be reconciled
through the Incarnation:

> The divine mandates in the world are not intended to con-
> sume man in endless conflicts; on the contrary, they are di-
> rected toward the whole man, as he stands in reality before
> God. . . . But this unity is achieved only when man allows
> himself to be confronted in Jesus Christ with the accomplished
> reality of the incarnation of God and of the reconciliation of
> the world with God in the crib, the cross and the resurrection
> of Jesus Christ. . . . The doctrine of the divine mandates
> threatens to lead to a perilous disintegration of man and of
> reality; yet it is precisely this doctrine which serves to confront
> man with the one and entire reality which is manifested to
> us in Jesus Christ. Thus here again all the lines converge in
> the reality of the body of Jesus Christ, in which God and man
> became one.[4]

Thus the intersections between religion and politics become the
crossroads at which the Christian confronts both the fullness of
God and the fullness of the world which God has made.

The philosopher Erich Kahler said during World War II
that "the central issue of our time is whether we believe there
is one human race with a common destiny, or whether we believe
only in a multiplicity of races and nations, warring against one
another in a meaningless conflict."[5] The search for meaning
in the midst of relentless international conflict has engaged both
religious and political leaders throughout the twentieth century.
Both theologies and political philosophies have made this unending strife the point of departure for new systems of thought.
Both dominie and diplomat have been seeking out threads of
identification with those who were arrayed against them in struggles of increasingly ultimate dimensions.

For truly universal religions like Christianity, there is an
unyielding imperative to identify not only with a transcendent
God nor simply with a national community: there is the third

dimension of a world community asserting its claims to human loyalty. The Christian is obliged by the commands of his faith, the security of his nation, and the suffering of human beings in every nation to devote his energies to the shaping of the political instruments of world community. Somehow, he must bring his piety and his patriotism into a triangular relationship with his new and universal loyalty. The radical monotheism of the late Richard Niebuhr specified the requirements of this loyalty: it is a loyalty to all men

> as bound together by a loyalty that is not only resident in them but transcends them. It is not only their loyalty to each other that makes them one realm of being, but the loyalty that comes from beyond them. . . . In radical monotheism my neighbor is my companion in being; though he is my enemy in some less than universal context the requirement is to love him.[6]

There is thus a fundamental reality to the world community which derives from the very source of its life, even though the political apparatus of that community may be crippled by power struggles.

THE RECONCILIATION OF POLITICS

The quest for common loyalties in the world community has assumed a variety of political and religious forms: Catholic Christendom, imperial conquest, international law, the League of Nations, the United Nations, the missionary movement, the ecumenical movement, cultural exchange, an international ethos. Sir Henry Maine, the English jurist, declared confidently in 1887 that the Christian nations were "bound together by the brighter light and the more definite sanction which Christianity has communicated to the ethical jurisprudence of the ancients and have established a law of nations peculiar to themselves. They form together a community united by religion, morals, and humanity." [7] This pious optimism of the generation before the holocaust of 1914-1918 had been encouraged by a relatively peaceful seventy years in Europe; it also harked back to a reality called Christendom which had dominated the Middle Ages and had fashioned the classical instruments of Western diplomacy: international law, the practices of negotiation, the dispatching of envoys and ambassadors to councils and courts. Even at the summit of Christendom, however, there was the split between the Roman Church and the Greek Church—and relentless hostility toward Moslem and pagan peoples. The reality of Christendom, limited at best, was eventually shattered by the pressures of modern nationalism.

International law still provides standards of conduct for the nations, but its identification with Christian sources and with imperial Western powers tends to undermine its authority in the East; indeed, international law is not always enforceable among the Christian nations of the West. It is in this context that the zeal of such American statesmen as Bryan, Wilson, and Dulles to reimpose a Christian international law must be seen as an embarrassment to other nations better adjusted to the decline of Christendom and more frankly seeking to advance their own interests.

One expression of the mission of America in the early 1900's was the attempt to Christianize and democratize relationships among states. When resistance to these righteous purposes was encountered, it was taken as proof of the iniquity of power politics and a summons to even greater efforts to convert the world. Only the extension of the American rule of law to the chaotic and cynical realm of diplomacy could secure world peace. Financed by such American industrialists as Andrew Carnegie, the peace movements campaigned for treaties of arbitration. In the period from 1900 to 1930, the government responded with a vast investment of time and trouble to negotiate 97 such agreements —90 bilateral, 7 multilateral. That these treaties, sanctioned so fervently by religious leaders, did not provide security either for the United States or for the world, is hardly necessary to report. Only two of them were ever invoked; it can be said of the others that they had "not the faintest effect on the development of the terrible wars and upheavals by which the first half of this century was marked." [8]

The League of Nations won, initially, a most earnest response from American Protestants. Every denomination except the Southern Baptists officially supported the League, and church members sent a shower of telegrams to the Senate Foreign Relations Committee and to individual senators. Methodism's Council of Bishops declared that "the League of Nations is an advance toward the period prophesied by the Hebrew prophet when men should not 'learn war any more.'" The Executive Committee of the Federal Council of Churches cabled Wilson at Paris to announce that the League was "the political expression of the Kingdom of God on earth." [9] Failure of the United States to join the League after having launched the crusade for it subjected the nation to a charge of hypocrisy as strong as the judgment of iniquity upon the nations of Europe had been in the first place.

The memory of the disillusionment, indifference, and isolationism of the interwar years prompted the vigorous campaign of the Dulles Commission to win mass support for the United Nations. Dulles and other Protestant leaders later came to regard that campaign as the turning point in persuading the Senate that the new international organization would have popular approval. One such leader reported in 1948 that "the influence of church-related groups in creating a public opinion favorable to the idea of the United Nations has been tremendous. Scores of notable church conferences, thousands of study groups in churches all over our land have given millions of people a Christian point of view on international relations." [10] The enthusiasm of that report is matched by the skepticism of Almond who acknowledged the element of truth in it: "The campaign for the United Nations has contained religious overtones and has been led by the guardians of the community conscience—teachers, clergy, and the various women's organizations." His concern was that the quality of support for the United Nations might rouse such "sanguine expectations" that the inevitable failures of the organization would produce a reaction of disillusionment.[11] There is a crusading brand of internationalism which boomerangs when its high hopes are frustrated by the stubborn realities of nationalism.

The San Francisco Conference made a notable effort to provide for the participation of non-governmental organizations,
including the churches. The access of Protestant groups to the
American delegation enabled them to exert some influence upon
the drafting of the United Nations Charter, particularly with
regard to human rights, the eventual freedom of colonial peoples,
the emphasis upon international law, and economic and social
co-operation. Long identified with underdeveloped countries
and their needs, Protestant churches have subsequently given
constant support to both U. N. and U. S. efforts in the fields of
economic and technical assistance. Foreign mission programs in
such practical matters as education, literacy, health, sanitation,
vocational training provided a fund of experience upon which
United Nations and official American policies could build. Hambidge's history of the Food and Agricultural Organization records that religious bodies pioneered in technical co-operation
and agricultural development and that Protestant-Catholic co-
operation had been noteworthy in these fields. Both the Vatican
and the World Council of Churches' Commission on International Affairs maintain consultative status with F.A.O.[12]

The World Council commission (CCIA) was largely the product of John Foster Dulles and brought to a common focus
several streams of ecumenical interest in international affairs.
On the eve of World War II, Dulles had attended the Oxford
Conference on Church, Community, and State in 1937, along
with such other Protestant leaders as Henry Smith Leiper, H. P.
VanDusen, John R. Mott, Henry Sloan Coffin, John Mackay,
and John C. Bennett. During the war, Sweden and Switzerland
served as neutral oases for the ecumenical movement as well as
for diplomats. Geneva became the headquarters for the Protestant underground, linking churches in Nazi-occupied countries
with those of the United States and Britain:

> Geneva was a city in which servants of the philanthropic
> societies, diplomats, resistance-leaders, refugees, and Church
> leaders of many nations met and helped each other to keep
> the lines of communication open. In some cases documents
> crossed the frontiers in diplomatic bags; in other cases through

the courier-service which the illegal press of the resistance movements had established between the various countries. Much of the material came in the form of tiny microfilms which might be hidden in a piece of shavingsoap or a fountain pen. In this way information constantly streamed through the World Council office and was passed on to the Churches through the Ecumenical Press Service or in less official ways.[13]

Paralleling the precarious development of a "World Council of Churches-in-process-of-formation," as it was known during the war years, the International Missionary Council had nurtured its own "witness in international relations, even unto death," as its Madras Conference had put it in 1938. Through the Protestant underground, an Orphaned Missions Fund was established: German missions in several places were cut off from their home country but were supported by Americans, Dutchmen, and Swedes. The practical ministries of the war years were continued after 1945 in the World Council's Department of Interchurch Aid and Service to Refugees. There was, however, a determination in both the W.C.C. and the I.M.C. to help shape future policy decisions—not just to provide relief after the outbreak of international violence.

Dulles was keenly interested in helping to create an ecumenical agency which could relate itself effectively to international decision-making. At Cambridge, England, in August, 1946, the CCIA was created. Five assumptions guided its formation: (1) technical skills are required if the churches are to exercise a responsible role in international relations; (2) a continuing day-to-day operation is necessary to supplement the work of ecclesiastical bodies which meet only periodically; (3) pronouncements are effective only as they are brought to bear at the time and place of political decisions; (4) specialized organization must be maintained for these functions; and (5) such organization must avoid compromising political entanglements.[14] With offices in New York, London, and Geneva, the CCIA recruited a membership of more than forty commissioners in almost as many countries: in addition to Dulles (who resigned when he became Secretary of State), prominent lay members have included Charles

Malik, Werner Kagi, Arnold Toynbee, R. A. Butler, and Frank Graham. The CCIA is affiliated with national commissions and other groups in more than 70 countries. As a "NGO" (non-governmental organization), its staff has regularly been in attendance at U.N. meetings, as well as meetings of foreign ministers, the Korean truce negotiations, and at other trouble spots.

If it cannot be said that CCIA often has a decisive influence upon national or international policies, it can be said that such a disinterested agency with broad international contacts can provide unique assistance in shaping many of the details of policy implementation and in improving the networks of personal relationships which often determine the success or failure of diplomacy. Because of this modest role and limited resources, the Commission has yet to establish a clear identity with public opinion in the United States and most other countries. Drs. O. Frederick Nolde and Richard M. Fagley, both Americans and serving respectively as director and executive secretary, have nevertheless gained great respect among both diplomats and churchmen for their professional competence in both international affairs and religion. They acknowledge the lack of local parish awareness of their work which, paradoxically, weakens their power while gaining a measure of privacy and flexibility. Nolde avoids the word "lobbying": there is no threatening reference to a "constituency of 170,000,000 people all over the world." The emphasis is upon "helping diplomats do a better job." [15]

The CCIA's influence is further weakened by the internal conflicts within Protestantism. The paramount role of Dulles in the early years and the predominance of an American staff have troubled both the staff itself and church leaders from other countries. Commission Chairman Sir Kenneth Grubb frankly observed in 1956 that the "enormous power" of the United States and the "considerable influence" of American Protestantism combine to "set the nature and shape the rules of international ecumenical discussion." [16] Another conflict is the irrepressible pacifist-non-pacifist tension. In its daily work, the CCIA staff feels compelled to proceed upon such non-pacifist assumptions as negotiation from strength and the insistence that disarmament procedures be multilateral. These assumptions and the charge of undue American influence were sharply focused in 1950 when the World Council's Central Committee endorsed United Nations military action in Korea. The Council statement, prepared by CCIA executive secretary Fagley and by Methodist Bishop G. Bromley Oxnam, was criticized by pacifists as well as by representatives from neutralist and Communist nations. From an opposite direction, former Commission member Reinhold Niebuhr and others have complained that CCIA work is based upon illusions and lacks the realistic approach of power politics. There is an internal political life within the churches as in all institutions which makes it impossible for all interests and all viewpoints to be satisfied all the time.

The "opinion gap" afflicts ecumenical agencies in even more acute form than denominational agencies. The ability of CCIA and related national commissions to influence mass opinion in the churches is not impressive. There are instructive parallels between the World Council of Churches and the United Nations. Both claim to be inclusive and representative bodies but are staffed by personnel who are more or less marginal to their constituencies. Ecumenical pronouncements on international affairs are manifestly in advance of public opinion at the parish level; United Nations proposals languish for lack of broad political support in member nations. Both the W.C.C. and the U.N. have only delegated, limited functions. Both agencies have only very limited resources with which to work: the U.N. budget is infinitesimal by comparison with national budgets and the W.C.C. budget does not compare with denominational budgets in the United States. Ecumenical and denominational specialists in international affairs are hemmed in by the boundaries of a new international elite which Brinton has characterized as

> a group of men and women skilled in the ways of co-operation among varied peoples, trained and practiced persons, an international elite not entirely divorced from national allegiance, but on the whole devoted to the task of getting in practice beyond the sovereign nation-state . . . The proportion of preachers and teachers among them may still be a bit excessive. They probably form too much of a coterie, if not a

sect, who see too much of one another at meetings, conferences, congresses and other places where the converted preach to the converted.[17]

There are also severe limits to Protestant influence in the very size and distribution of Protestantism in the world. Christianity as a whole is a minority group on the world scene; it is challenged not only by secularism and by Communism but also by a renewed missionary zeal in such world religions as Islam and Hinduism which have helped to fuel nationalist revolutions in Asia and Africa. There is a tendency for American Christians to pretend to a religious as well as a political sovereignty in the world—to exaggerate the weight and power of Christianity in the world. A symptom of this pretense is the moralistic use of the very word "Christian" which may prove embarrassing on diplomatic occasions. During a United Nations review of the Arab-Israeli dispute—in which religious sensitivities have been inflamed so often—former U. S. Delegate Warren Austin arose solemnly and urged the quarreling Moslem and Jewish delegates to settle their differences "in a spirit of Christian charity." (This unfortunate remark was later stricken from the record, at Mr. Austin's request.)

A more serious faith conflict occurred during U. N. discussions of the proposed Declaration of Human Rights in 1948. Article 18 of the Charter, in the preparation of which CCIA participation had been conspicuous, provided an essentially American Protestant definition of the fullness of religious freedom. Various amendments were proposed in the General Assembly. Delegate Pavlov of the Soviet Union moved the addition of the clause "in accordance with the laws of the country concerned and the requirements of public morality." Moslem Delegate Baroody of Saudi Arabia, after sharply criticizing Christian missionaries as the "forerunners of political intervention," asked for an amendment which would restrict the definition to "freedom of thought, conscience, and religion." In final Assembly voting, both amendments were defeated 45-4 with 4 abstentions.[18]

Protestantism is a minority within a minority because its total constituency is smaller than that of Catholicism. Catholics number about 500,000,000, Protestants 250,000,000, Orthodox bodies 125,000,000. Denominations represented in the World Council of Churches constitute less than 10 per cent of the world's population and less than 30 per cent of the Christian total. The distribution is such that Protestantism is weakest where international conflicts are actually or potentially most acute. As Grubb has noted, this factor seriously hampers Protestant influence in the pivotal Middle East. While the international dimensions of the ecumenical fellowship accord it certain strategic advantages, those advantages can be overestimated: "Christian people talk about the World Church being the new fact of our time, and it is quite true that the Church is there, but there is an aspect of this talk which is merely a whistling to keep up one's courage in the dark." [19] While it may be premature to describe our generation as living in the post-Christian era, no amount of missionary zeal or evangelical effort is likely to restore the term "Christendom" to realistic usage in our time.

An alternative effort has been undertaken since the Oxford Conference of 1937 to identify a common ethos or common foundation of moral convictions which transcends both religious and political boundaries. Nine general principles for an "international ethos" were tentatively advanced and accepted by the World Council of Churches at its Evanston Assembly in 1954:

(1) All power carries responsibility and all nations are trustees of power which should be used for the common good.

(2) All nations are subject to moral law, and should strive to abide by the accepted principles of international law to develop this law and to enforce it through common actions.

(3) All nations should honor their pledged word and international agreements into which they have entered.

(4) No nation in an international dispute has the right to be sole judge in its own cause or to resort to war to advance its policies, but should seek to settle disputes by direct negotiation or by submitting them to conciliation, arbitration, or judicial settlement.

(5) All nations have an obligation to insure universal security and to this end should support measures designed to deny victory to a declared aggressor.

(6) All nations should recognize and safeguard the inherent dignity, worth and essential rights of the human person, without distinction as to race, sex, language or religion.

(7) Each nation should recognize the rights of every other nation, which observes such standards, to live by and proclaim its own political and social beliefs, provided that it does not seek by coercion, threat, infiltration or deception to impose these on other nations.

(8) All nations should recognize an obligation to share their scientific and technical skills with peoples in less developed regions, and to help the victims of disaster in other lands.

(9) All nations should strive to develop cordial relations with their neighbors, encourage friendly cultural and commercial dealings, and join in creative international efforts for human welfare.[20]

This is American Protestant internationalism at its best. It does not, however, transcend the most serious ethical, ideological, and political differences in the present world; it represents, rather, an extension of the Puritan ethos of the American people into an international ethos of the same principles. Even within American Protestantism, these principles are challenged. The Wilsonian doctrine of collective security which is implicit in them is rejected, for opposite reasons, by both pacifists and "realists." The pacifist objects to the use of military force to resist aggression. The "realist" challenges the assumptions of collective security with regard to the definability of aggression; he also questions whether all nations have the interests or the capacities to resist aggression.[21] What is more obvious is that Wilsonian legalism is unacceptable to Marxist ideology and to such Asian nations as India—witness the military occupation of Goa by India in 1961. Walter Muelder suggests that international law is more the fruit than the source of world community. "An international ethos must emerge from all the groups which participate significantly in world society. No one nation, group of nations, economic society, or religious body can provide such an ethos for others." [22]

There is an existential creation of common values which takes place quite beyond the efforts of religious or political leaders to control. What most Christians and most Communists have yet to perceive is the extent to which a common ethos transcending both has been generated by historic developments within the United States and the Soviet Union. Arnold Toynbee has imaginatively merged Russian socialism and American free enterprise into a "Russo-American goddess" wearing an identical suit of clothes:

> And if you identify the goddess with her dress, the name that you give her will depend on which way out you make her wear her suit. In the eyes of any citizen of the Old World, this Russo-American suit of clothes might look peculiar because its material is economic stuff, and to dress a goddess in that is something new in the history of religion. At some place and time, human beings have worshiped almost everything under the sun: animals, trees, crops, thunderbolts. But this is surely the first time in history that anyone has ever worshiped systems of economic production and distribution.[23]

The essential difference between the two systems—and according to Toynbee this is an "enormous" difference—is the degree of spiritual freedom in America. The common materialism of the Russian and the American systems raises, however, some new ethical dilemmas for Christianity.

Schematically, the following components of a common Russo-American ethos may be specified:

1. Both modern nations were created out of violent revolution and retain a certain revolutionary fervor.

2. Both nations, from the depths of national character, have projected a moralistic ideology into the campaign for world opinion.

3. Both nations occupy large land masses not easily conquered and tending to perpetuate a tradition of isolationism and suspicion.

4. Both nations are led by Caucasians and Westerners (although a favorite ideological maneuver of the Soviets is to trap Americans into a pattern of "East-West" thinking so that Russians may be identified with the non-Caucasian peoples of the East—notwithstanding Soviet sovereignty over the Caucasus!).

5. Both nations include large non-Caucasian populations who

provide sources of both identification and conflict with other nations.

6. Both nations have been transformed from rural agrarian societies into urbanized and industrialized societies.

7. Both economic systems have been relentlessly driven by technological revolutions and give high priority to scientific values.

8. Both political systems, professing a disdain for the state as such, have become increasingly centralized and bureaucratized (compare Jefferson's "least government" with Marx's promise that the state will "wither away").

9. Both nations, professing an abhorrence of peacetime armed forces, have become highly militarized.

10. Both societies, professing an egalitarian ideology, have developed class inequalities which can only be rationalized with much difficulty.

11. Both governments lack continuity with the stable diplomatic traditions of the nineteenth century and reveal a certain lack of sophistication and maturity in their diplomatic conduct.

12. Both political systems subject foreign policy to a high degree of party interference militating against the security and autonomy of professional diplomats.

These similarities are not necessarily hopeful for the resolution of American-Russian tensions. The very fact of similarity sometimes imparts a peculiar intensity to personal or social conflict. Moveover, such parallels tend to alienate neutral nations who may not share the same values and who feel threatened by both systems. The challenge to Christian ethics is to avoid any simple or uncritical identification with national ideologies and yet retain a relevance within both national and international arenas. That relevance includes generating a creative ferment out of which truly universal political values and loyalties may emerge.

It is not enough to support international law, the United Nations, and the ecumenical movement: the builders of a world community must work with the national communities which history has provided them. Too many "good people" in the United States assume the anti-political, anti-nationalist stance of official priests, promoters, guardians, guides, and cheerleaders for the United Nations.

Perhaps the most thoughtful encounter of this paradoxical relationship between nationalism and internationalism has been taking place within the missionary movement in the past decade. The demand for indigenous leadership in mission fields and the explosive nationalism which imposes that demand have raised critical issues for mission strategy which shadow the problems of diplomacy. Kitagawa has called attention to the unwitting parallels between mission bureaucracy and the bureaucracy of colonial administration by imperial governments. The basic pattern of control historically has been domination by foreign boards and societies. Missionary bureaucracy, like all forms of bureaucracy, has tended toward an in-group defensiveness and a rigidity in the face of change.[24] A recent awakening to the hazards of missionary colonialism has, in fact, led to significant changes in mission administration.

It is not only the pattern of control that is at issue: it is also the ethical meaning of nationalism. We are not likely to appreciate the meaning of nationalism in the new political communities of Asia and Africa if we do not have a profound appreciation of the significance of nationalism in American experience. Canon Warren has been critical of a tendency toward an uprooted and sentimental internationalism in some mission thinking. Noting with approval the call of the Willingen Conference of the International Missionary Council in 1952 for international mission teams, he nevertheless protested against denationalizing missionaries. Invoking the doctrine of the Incarnation, Warren declared: "At least a part of the 'foreigner's' offering lies *not* in the fact that he is proclaiming eternal truths but that in himself and in his *nationality* he is a demonstration that the Eternal can enter history and transform it." Nationalism must be understood as "the self-conscious assertion by a people of its own individuality in relation to other peoples." *Internationalism* is "not the negation of nationalism but its fulfilment in the community of nations." [25] The missionary, while he is uniquely exposed to nationalist tensions, has a special opportunity to serve as a two-way ambassador who remains deeply identified with both the country of his origin and the country of his work. This double-identification provides built-in correctives against the moral pretense and national self-righteousness which have contributed so much to international violence in modern history.

That a nation can and must be the vehicle of universal purposes is a truth which skepticism and cynicism dare not destroy; that a nation tempted to attach universal sanctions to its own interests can be the source of barbaric international violence is a truth which all of its leaders dare not forget. The political truth in various forms of the classical Christian doctrine of the Covenant is that nationalism and universalism must not be regarded as polar opposites but that they stand in a relation of mutual and positive fulfillment. If some American statesmen and their followers have revealed the excesses to which the Calvinistic version of the Covenant may lead, they have also revealed the public energies which may be released through a people convinced of a missionary destiny which transcends the cruder assertions of national self-interest. There is a missionary component of American foreign policy which must be allowed to retain its ethical vitality. That component may be the world's best hope that the struggle for peace and the struggle for freedom will continue side-by-side. The deepest purposes of the American nation belong to a world-community-in-process-of-becoming. American policy at its best is the incarnation of both national interests and those universal values which give meaning to national existence itself. It is based, as Walt Rostow has expressed it, upon "the conviction that the adventure of America has a meaning and relevance for the world as a whole." [26]

THE RECONCILIATION OF RELIGION

The nature of religious influence upon American policy is not simply a matter of external relationships between church and state: it depends, finally, upon the interior resources of the church itself. Protestantism, as the largest private constituency within the American public, has unique opportunities and heavy obligations in the processes by which that public shapes foreign policy. Protestant points of access have typically been more numerous than Protestants have themselves perceived. Their influence has been erratic and undisciplined because they have not possessed either the ethical wholeness or the practical wisdom to understand that influence. Fundamental to that lack of understanding has been an inability to come to realistic terms with the meaning of conflict. It is when that meaning is grasped that Protestantism may be prepared to release its special energies under the sustained disciplines of new strategies in the public arena. Together, such strategies for the management of conflict require an integrity of relationship between the inner life of the church and the outward witness of the church. There is no point in the church's life that is entirely separable from the life of the world to which the church brings its ministry of reconciliation.

The strategies of conflict, understood positively as well as negatively, may be termed the institutionalization of conflict. That jaw-breaking term is simply an indication that creative conflict requires planning and procedures. The institutionalization of conflict is not the process by which conflict is avoided or repressed or compartmentalized: it is the process by which disciplines of action make conflict serve redemptive purposes in the life of the church and the world. It is not the necessary opposite of co-operation: it is the precondition of any kind of co-operation which is truly vital.

The church requires new strategies of orientation to conflict in all dimensions of its work, including ministerial training, Christian education, pastoral care, lay activities, family life, missions, church administration—in addition to the more obvious field of social action. A persistent theme in this book has been the historic significance of the church's latent influence on world politics: the influence which may have been unintentional from the standpoint of social action and which may not even have been detected by religious leaders—but which bears the weight of dynamic religious energies nonetheless.

i. Theological education and world politics

Protestant elites can react either with resentment or with intelligent planning to a barrage of requests from political scientists and policy-makers that churches strive to make their influence more self-conscious and more dependable in the public arena. Those requests have not yet been heard by many church leaders who are in a position to make a difference in the quality of ministerial training. This is more than a problem of formal ethical orientation: it is a problem of making religious leaders perceptive and skillful participants in the process of opinion-formation. That process, it must be relentlessly repeated, is never very far from the deepest psychic realities of the human spirit. Public opinion, both by design and by default, brings the dominant values of a free society to bear upon national policy. Religious leaders have always wanted to believe that they were the custodians of those values: they should be awakened, in this age that they call secular, to the continuing vitality of the religious and idealistic currents in American opinion.

Perhaps the most notable plea for improving the quality of religious participation in public opinion was voiced by Gabriel Almond more than a decade ago. Almond did not suggest an assault upon mass opinion (a "crusade") through the churches: he directed attention to the curricula of theological seminaries. Ministers serve, whether they know it or not, at key points in the political process as bearers of moral and political idealism. They have tended, however, to "contribute to American moral dualism; they are responsible in part for the persistence of instability in American opinion. They set up aspirations which cannot be fulfilled, and inculcate principles of conduct which cannot be effective." Almond proposed that seminary education face up to "political reality" with courses which confront "the real problems of military and political security." [27] Almond's judgment of theological education has been supported by a 1961 study undertaken by Sutherlin, who reported an increasing climate of awareness of international issues in the seminaries, but little implementation in the curriculum.[28]

It is only within the integrity of the total ministry—and primarily as men are prepared for the ministry by theological seminaries—that the ethical and practical aspects of opinion leadership may be brought together most significantly. Fortunately, many Protestant seminaries are located in the nation's liveliest and most influential centers of foreign policy study and discussion: New York, Boston-Cambridge, Washington, Chicago, and others. These seminaries have vast and largely unexploited opportunities to reconcile the relevant theological and secular disciplines, to foster a genuine dialogue between theologians and political scientists, between pastors and policy-makers.

More than the mutual exposure of ethics and foreign policy is required: both of these fields need to be more fully exposed to the behavioral fields of public opinion and propaganda. The evangelical propagation of the faith has more to learn from the study of propaganda than religious leaders have yet appreciated. The preaching, educational, and action ministries of the church are addressed to the same public which propagandists and advertisers seek to influence. It is not that the clergy need to be made more effective manipulators of public opinion: the need is precisely the opposite. Only by exploring the ways in which opinion may be manipulated and by detecting the unwitting conspiracy of religion in that manipulation may Christian ethics be effectively lifted above the ideologies of party, class, and nation. Ideology has become, pre-eminently in the United States, a tool for the manipulation of public opinion by competing interest groups—clamoring and competing moralists, as we have earlier called them. Such techniques of propaganda study as "thematic analysis" and awareness of "boomerang effect" are directly relevant to the communication of the Gospel. Responsible communication, in the churches or anywhere else, requires some knowledge of the behavior of communication systems.

Perhaps the most sophisticated approach to religious elites in the field of foreign policy discussion is being employed by the Council on Religion and International Affairs (formerly the Church Peace Union). Since 1957, the CRIA (not to be confused with CCIA) has conducted seminars in New York and various regional centers in which clergy and lay participants focus upon the theme of ethics and foreign policy. The CRIA also has held a series of Washington consultations for advanced specialists and publishes a modest monthly journal, *Worldview*. As an interfaith body, the council provides a common forum for Protestants, Catholics, and Jews. Such a group has only a marginal relationship to the power structures of Protestantism, however, and cannot yet claim to have significantly influenced either mass opinion or theological education.

Most seminaries are not prepared to furnish the faculty, to make the curricular adjustments, and to engage in the secular negotiations with political science and international relations which would be required to improve the preparation of ministers for their inescapable service at key points in the political process. Mounting pressures upon faculty and curricula, deep-seated inhibitions concerning the separation of church and state, the risks of public misunderstanding and criticism, the suspicion that theological education is already too heavily steeped in non-theological studies, anxiety at the prospect of exposure to competent secular scholars—these are some of the obstacles to a ready response to Almond's plea. But they are obstacles which the apocalyptic demands of contemporary world politics must be allowed to overcome.

Where a seminary finds itself in a metropolitan university community which is a center of foreign policy studies—again, New York, Boston, Washington, Chicago come to mind—that seminary has the best opportunity to marshal the resources for a program of political ethics and international relations. Teaching and research might be conducted in such areas as the following: (1) theological issues in contemporary political thought; (2) religion and politics in American society; (3) public opinion and foreign policy; (4) ethics and United States foreign policy; (5) politics and policy-making as vocations; (6) world religions and world politics; (7) Christianity and Communism; and (8) religious strategy in world affairs. In an earlier time, these fields might have seemed on the remote periphery of Christian concern. In the 1960's, all of them are sucked into the vortex of crucial forces and events.

ii. Laymen and domestic diplomacy

Ministers and laymen together share a responsibility with policy-makers in the realm of domestic diplomacy, which might be defined as the nurture of the body politic in the interests of the nation as a whole; or, as the cultivation of the political and pre-political gardens in which creative national policies may be planted and may grow to fruitful maturity. Concretely, domestic diplomacy means working with the political parties and the pressure groups which tend to dominate policy decisions in the United States. It is on this domestic front that the national religion is so constantly subjected to ideological manipulation and so readily exploited to fan mass hostilities. It is not only the preachers who have generated moral indignation in the American psyche: business, labor, farm, veterans, and super-patriotic groups join some politicians in bombarding each other (as well as Communists) with a vitriolic hate which so often hides genuine political issues behind a fog of free-floating mass hostility. (Only last evening, I attended a public meeting at which a prominent businessman fervently prayed for "God's help in an all-out crusade to destroy Kennedy liberalism which is condemning our children to a life of Communist slavery.") Unless laymen learn to detect—and to resist—this inflaming of moral indignation as a weapon of political and economic conflict, there will be no chance for a reasonable debate over the national interest. A nation which becomes accustomed to such righteous venom in its internal political life is all too prepared to unload that poison upon other nations when international conflict develops. One of the practical maxims of the institutionalization of conflict is to shift energies from phony and unrealistic conflicts to genuine and realistic conflicts. (Moral indignation over the Supreme Court's school prayer decision was most conspicuous among those who had resented the court's desegregation decision.)

Protestantism has a rich heritage in the ministry of the laity which has yet to be seriously applied to the political responsibilities of American churchmen. Laymen are habitually detailed to such organizational jobs as building trustees, fund-raisers, and membership-recruiters—with an overlay of nostalgic evangelism —so that the substantive areas of church program are left to the preachers and the women. Preacher-and-female-dominated Christian education, missions, and social action are arrayed against entrenched and defensive laymen who are zealously preoccupied with institutional preservation. (This brings the conception of the "opinion gap" down to the existential earth!) This line-up thwarts political education and action in the churches and leaves secular pressure groups to which laymen belong without a radical challenge from prophetic Christian doctrines. This line-up also reinforces the desire to avoid controversial issues of any kind in the church: the fear of "splitting the church" is continually exploited to dull the cutting edge of the Gospel. Laymen need to be reconstituted into vocational circles and study groups which, under church auspices, come to terms both with the fullness of the Gospel and with the requirements of what German laymen call "civil courage." A section of the final report of the Evanston Assembly in 1954 began with this proclamation:

> The time has come to make the ministry of the laity explicit, visible and active in the world. The real battles of the faith today are being fought in factories, shops, offices and farms, in political parties and government agencies, in countless homes, in the press, radio and television, in the relationship of nations. Very often it is said that the church should "go into these spheres"; but the fact is that the church is already in these spheres in the persons of its laity.[29]

That proclamation is at once faithful to a great Reformation doctrine and most relevant to contemporary Christian strategy. In American society, especially, the elites of government, politics, and the economy are already within the church. It is these religious people who need to discover what the ministry of the laity is all about.

There are fundamentals of ethical and political education which only the churches can interpret adequately. These fundamentals have to do with lay vocations and with the moral qualities of secular groups—the collective realities which provide the unofficial structure of the body politic. Some of these fundamentals are implicit in the theoretical architecture of this study: how to express the absoluteness of Christian loyalty in the midst of worldly conflicts. Training and skill are required for the management of conflict. Three of these fundamentals may be mentioned briefly: (a) controversy over both the ends and means of policy; (b) compromise in making group decisions; and (c) consensus in sustaining a responsible policy. Such words as "controversy" and "compromise" ought to be positive terms in the Christian vocabulary. It is only the moralistic distortion of Protestant ideology which makes them bad words and which rationalizes the escape from these responsibilities of a free society. The ministry of reconciliation was made for these realities of controversy, compromise, and consensus. Controversy is a precondition of both political freedom and spiritual vitality; partisanship of some kind is absolutely indispensable. Christians ought to be specially equipped both to advocate their own convictions forthrightly and to listen to and learn from those who hold opposite convictions. The trouble with crusades is that they claim the whole truth, beget intolerance and bitterness, and deprive the crusaders themselves of the chance to discover their ignorance before it is too late. Compromise is a process of mutual adjustment which goes on in every human institution, including the family and the church. Compromise is less often a "moral sell-out" in politics than many Puritans realize: it is frequently a very practical ministry of reconciliation among competing interests which opens the way to public progress. Consensus is often the best approximation of domestic peace and non-violence which a society can achieve. Consensus is the minimum fund of common values which keeps a body politic from disintegrating completely.

Domestic diplomacy employs the disciplines of controversy, compromise, and consensus to manage political conflicts in the national interest and in the interests of peace in the world. To manage conflicts is to manage the realities of power which are the essence of politics. All politics is power politics: all politics generates tension. "The eternal problem of politics, national or international, domestic or foreign, is not to do away with power but to tame it, to control it, to confine it within legitimate channels."[30] Defining the legitimate channels for the exercise of power is inherently an ethical task as well as a political one. Schuman confronts the political ethics of Protestant America with this double challenge:

> The age-old quest of decent and reasoning men for an ethics broader than the in-group may usefully be regarded as a double problem: that of *reducing* within every community the volume of insecurities, tensions, and aggressions seeking destructive release, and of *achieving* a symbolism and value-system sufficiently universal to make possible universal fellowship through uniformity of emotional identifications. However variously expressed, this in truth has been the mission of all universalists, social reformers, prophets of righteousness, and preachers of God.[31]

That is the statement of a political scientist and not a theologian. It charts the political dimensions of a realistic ministry of the laity through American churches. It suggests that religious energies must do more than promote wartime sacrifice and peacetime privacy. It calls, rather, for an unrelenting heroism in facing up to those domestic problems—economic, racial, educational— which at all times call for the highest degree of creative nationalism. It also calls for boldness and imagination in linking the American people with the political struggles of other peoples on remote continents.

iii. Family life as pre-politics

The orientation of persons to the meaning of power is the highest task given to political ethics. But the psychic properties of power clamor for the recognition that the decisive experiences in the meaning of power occur in the very early years of life. No program of formal instruction can make up for a lack of personal nurture in the meaning of power, primarily within the family arena. The qualities of experience in making decisions, attitudes toward authority and responsibility, habits of controversy and compromise, loyalty to and identification with larger interests than the self—all of these aspects of the meaning of power are schooled in persons long before, if ever, they are aware that they are being schooled. The family is a vital pre-political institution, as studies of national character in Germany and Japan make clear—and as studies of voting behavior in the United States demonstrate. More important, the family is the first power-system experienced by members of society.

The family life planning of Protestantism, like the programs of lay activities, tends toward an artificial segregation of the family from the world. The "togetherness" theme has produced somewhat sentimental family devotions and family recreation, the effect of which may be simply to help white, middle class suburban families to escape the most crucial conflicts which confront the American nation—and to feel good while escaping. Ralph Lazarus, a distinguished businessman, has described suburban family life as a "social incubator" in communities surrounded by walls which

> tend to keep out everyone not belonging to a single economic class, whether they be the walls of a low-cost housing project, of a Levittown or Sunny Acres, or the zoning walls of Darien, Conn., or Grosse Pointe, Mich. Outside these walls is America, with its teeming multitudes, its color, vitality, conflict, and choice. In the process of building man's first suburban civilization, we are segregating our society into tens of thousands of economic ghettos. . . . We are developing what I call Classville, USA. . . . We cannot expect children to walk straight out of a social incubator and cope with a world of national and international conflict.[32]

The family mirrors all of the world's problems. Dinner-table conversation is not unrelated to the prejudices and the animosities which divide the human race. Family budget-planning is not separable from the hunger and homelessness, the disease and illiteracy of millions of other families. Protestantism has generally failed to recognize that there is an organic relationship between the family and society—indeed, among all human institutions, including church and state—which must be apprehended as basic to Christian ethics. Through pastoral imagination and through a more prophetic program of Christian education, the need of American families for meaningful functions can be matched with many of the needs of far-away people and places. Children who grow up in homes where CARE packages are prepared, international foster children or pen pals adopted, visitors of other nationalities and races welcome, parents involved in causes in which they deeply believe—such children may become more resourceful adults in decades of international conflict than those whose homes are only conventionally religious. Families are strategic points of access for both long-range political nurture and for the more urgent and sacrificial tasks required of compassionate people in a world of privation and hate.

iv. War and peace: a divided witness still

There is no Biblical promise that the earth itself will last forever. Great powers are now preoccupied with preparation for a warfare of earth-obliterating violence. Pacifists are convinced that such warfare and the threat to wage it are not to be justified by Christian ethics. Non-pacifists acknowledge the risks of nuclear war and of a deterrence policy, but they regard these risks as a lesser evil than the conquest of the world by Communism. Neither the pacifist nor the non-pacifist is entitled to confidence that his policy will succeed. A national policy of non-violence is no guarantee against mass destruction; a national policy of nuclear retaliation is no guarantee against the triumph of Communism. Either policy could lead to war or to Communist conquest—or both—or neither. We simply do not know what is going to happen to our world.

The tension between pacifists and non-pacifists within the church incarnates the conception of conflict which has shaped this entire discussion of religion and politics. In some respects, the tension is valuable: neither group embodies the whole of Christian ethics. Pacifists tend to emphasize the absoluteness of Christian loyalty, the conflict between church and state, the need for a sanctuary from violence and for a ministry of reconciliation.

Non-pacifists tend to emphasize the imperatives of political responsibility and the inevitability of political conflict. Pacifists risk a complete political alienation as well as the disintegration of the political community. Non-pacifists risk a squandering of the creative tensions in the Christian witness as well as the destruction of the political community. Together, pacifists and non-pacifists provide mutual correctives and encompass the range of the six inherent functions of religion in world politics. It is unfortunate that estrangement between pacifists and non-pacifists often prevents their working together on many matters of common concern. Not all of the issues of foreign policy hang on a speculative "yes" or "no" answer to the question of actually using nuclear weapons. In fact, the very success of either nuclear deterrence or non-violence is at best a reprieve to work on the many non-military problems of human affairs. Here are some of the elements of a tentative Christian consensus in international relations—a consensus which transcends the pacifist-non-pacifist divide and which is entitled to the sanction of both groups:

1. Resistance to ideological fanaticism in the Cold War and a concern for the hazards of national self-righteousness.
2. Rejection of various forms of neo-isolationism.
3. Recognition of the challenge posed by the social, economic, and ideological appeals of Communism.
4. Insistence that a military policy preoccupied with the threat of all-out nuclear war not only intensifies the threat of war but obscures the nature of most present and probable international conflicts, especially in Asia and Africa.
5. Awareness of the need to minimize the possibility of accidental war which could result from technical miscues, mental breakdown of military personnel, or the adventurous use of nuclear weapons by third powers.
6. Attention to non-military factors—political, social, psychological—as preconditions of both national security and world community.
7. Support for effective economic and technical assistance to other nations.

8. Perception of the international consequences of such domestic problems as race relations and agricultural production.
9. Concern to understand the nature of human violence and the compulsions and aversions which attend violence in public opinion.
10. Acknowledgement that the elements of risk and sacrifice accompany any conceivable foreign policy.

Harvey Seifert has charged that Christians generally have lacked a capacity for sustained attention to the long-range problems of foreign policy. This is a failing common to both pacifists and non-pacifists:

> If we weighed distant goals more heavily, we would insist that present choices include elements which might make even better choices possible in the future. Neither the pacifist nor the participant has dealt fully with the goal of peace until, in addition to nonparticipation or participation in present wars, he also invests energy in some movement aimed at the future elimination of war. His dimension of concern then includes a program designed to abolish for future generations the tragic decision to which he is now limited. . . . It should prevent too hasty an acceptance of the compromise which first commended itself.[33]

Whatever else the ministry of reconciliation may mean in world affairs, it is a radical commission to become involved in unceasing strategies to relieve suffering, injustice, hostility, fear—all potent causes of international violence.

Both pacifists and non-pacifists have performed distinctive ministries which must continue. Between the two world wars, the Quaker International Service, a little publicized operation with headquarters in Geneva, demonstrated the unique capacity of pacifist diplomacy in conflict situations. The Service maintained embassies and ambassadors in such cities as Paris, Berlin, Vienna, and Rome. These centers provided opportunities for negotiation when regular political channels were blocked; they were widely trusted across national boundaries when suspicion hampered the work of other agencies. While such ambassadors were under no illusions about their ability to control political forces in Europe, they provided an array of humanitarian services until full-scale war resumed. Harsh treatment of political prisoners in several countries was alleviated; emergency relief supplies were provided the populations of a number of cities; exchange family visits and study conferences crossed both the Franco-German and the Polish-German frontiers.[34]

The most distinctive ministry of reconciliation currently being performed by some non-pacifists is their identification with the human problems of the military community. It is primarily through concerned non-pacifists that the degree of ethical concern among military leaders themselves is appreciated; the technical problems of military decision-making explored; the variety of policy alternatives among military thinkers understood. There is an experience of alienation for many persons in the armed forces which is the consequence of their separation from more natural communities, their immediate identification with weapons of mass destruction, and their ethical tension which calls for pastoral sensitivity and a restraint upon the amount of moral hostilities unleashed against "militarism." From this difficult ministry emerges a new kind of challenge to those pacifists and others for whom "militarism" is only an angry word: those who are most deeply concerned about war should be those who have the fullest comprehension of the problems of the military community.

v. The internal arena of conflict

The ministry of reconciliation knows no concrete reality in institutions as such. Beyond all strategies for the institutionalization of conflict are the strategies of the soul: the internalization of conflict. It is in the private arena of the inner life that the claims of faith confront the claims of the world in a perpetual warfare.

The final logic of political ethics for the Christian is that his most perfect expression of transcendent loyalty is only to be found in that arena of conflict in which it is most difficult for him to express that loyalty. Only as he subjects himself to the secular world in its law and force and controversy can he come to know the political meaning of the Crucifixion which is prio

to, but fulfilled in, the ultimate meaning of the Crucifixion.
The six-fold typology set forth in these pages does not solve
the problems of war and peace. It is only an heuristic framework
to encourage historical perception and ethical wholeness. Practi-
cally, it commends six ethical and historical imperatives for
Christian statesmanship:

1. Radical faithfulness to the Living Center of the religious
   fellowship and the open communication of the meaning of
   that loyalty both within and beyond the fellowship.
2. Profound identification with one's own and other national
   communities and with the burdens of those who serve as
   trustees of national heritage in their public vocations.
3. A proper regard for political conflict as inevitable and as a
   vital necessity in the service of both freedom and faith.
4. A prophetic role of criticism within one's own political community, with care not to express or encourage a general aversion to political life and its tensions.
5. A personal ministry to both participants in and victims of
   political conflict, both domestic and international.
6. Directing the energies of constituents to forces making for the
   resolution of conflict and engaging them in sacrificial disciplines which relate organically to those forces.

Beyond these practical tasks, the Christian statesman will
need to articulate a "theology of conflict" which expresses the
radical apprehension of both the most violent and destructive
forces which can be released in human struggle and of the most
redeeming and creative forces which can only be released in human struggle. The prophetic tradition of the Scriptures possessed
such a theology. What is tragically or triumphantly true in the
life of nations is not less true in all human communities or in
the persons who comprise them: there is an internal arena of
struggle which participates in every external arena of struggle.
The internal arena must generate the power of moral absolutism
—but it must also contrive the disciplines which control that
power, which focus its energies, which limit its perversions, which
correct its abuses.

"Idealists" have all too often failed to recognize the inevitable and pervasive qualities of conflict. Their habitual drive is to abolish conflict, to eliminate tensions, to solve problems which can never be fully solved. The most enthusiastic idealists of every generation are subject to disillusionment when the demonic propensities of the conflicts they sought to avoid take their toll of life and virtue.

"Realists," who recognize the fact of conflict, are always tempted to interpret it by their own dogmas about the nature of man, the nature of history, the nature of evil—but their dogmatic preoccupation is misplaced. Radical monotheism cannot permit the erection of rigid dogmas concerning man, history, or evil because every such dogma becomes an idolatrous rival for the exclusive loyalty which belongs to God alone. These dogmas chronically blind the "realists" to the creative possibilities of man's moral response in history. While they have proclaimed the transcendence of God, they have not known how fully transcendent He is and how mysteriously His works are done. They have had very little to say about the meaning of the Incarnation and the Church as the Body of Christ. But it is that dogmatic core which truly nourishes and sustains the ministry of reconciliation.

Conflict—the actual and potential opposition of wills, human and divine—is not simply the consequence of evil or the ambivalence of man's nature or the intransigence of history. It is the divinely given precondition of all meaningful human freedom and all meaningful human responsibility. There is no reconciliation without conflict. But conflict itself has no ultimate status before the One God: it is only His arrangement for the bringing of all His creatures into the fullest possible fellowship with Himself. Man's separation from God and from his fellows is not an inherently evil fact: it is essential to his salvation as a free being.

Decision-making, for the Christian, has no inherent properties which dictate a less-than-faithful decision, whether in families or in foreign policies. That there are tensions to be borne is not the final word to be said. Political ethics, for the Christian, can have no other source than the message of reconciliation and all of the inherent requirements of that message, according to which he must be an ambassador for Christ.

As the individual Christian identifies himself with all human conflicts and internalizes them within his own being, he helps to resolve the tensions among international political and religious systems which have combined to assault men and women, young people and children, with hostility and guilt, pain and sorrow and death, through long immemorial centuries— but which have become so demonic in these latest generations. This may be the new kind of Christian for whom the world is waiting: the person whose way of life is to take up all of the world's struggles within himself, and there, upon that inner battleground, by a Power which is ready to use every battle creatively, to win the greatest of victories. But such a definition has, after all, a familiar ring: "For in him all the fullness of God was pleased to dwell, and through him to reconcile to himself all things, whether on earth or in heaven, making peace by the blood of his cross."[35]

Appendix

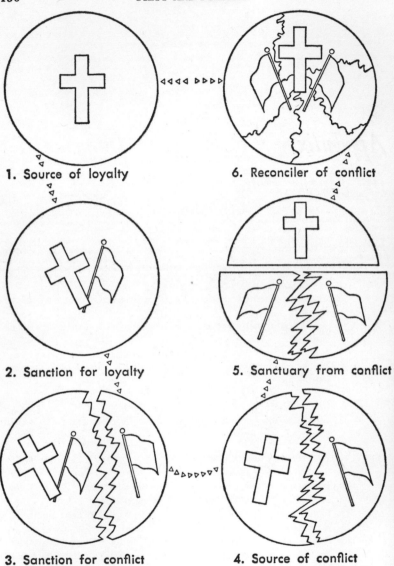

1. Source of loyalty

6. Reconciler of conflict

2. Sanction for loyalty

5. Sanctuary from conflict

3. Sanction for conflict

4. Source of conflict

**A TYPOLOGY OF RELIGIOUS ACTION
IN THE POLITICAL ARENA**

An Inventory of Religious Influence in World Politics

I. International influences

  A. Relationships among religious communities

    1. Source of supranational loyalties
    2. Source of group loyalties co-operating with other world religions
    3. Source of group loyalties conflicting with other world religions
    4. System of international communications
    5. Agency for education and information concerning international affairs
    6. Relief from the suffering occasioned by participation in international conflict
    7. Sanction for non-participation by religious persons in world politics

  B. Relationships among nation-states

    8. Source of international law
    9. Intensifier of national hostility to other peoples
    10. Reducer of national hostility to other peoples
    11. Component of emerging ideologies among foreign peoples
    12. Rejection of emerging ideologies among foreign peoples
    13. Source of division in the body politic in foreign countries
    14. Agency of the government in the formation or execution of policy
    15. Specific object of foreign policy
    16. Action supplementing official policy goals
    17. Action antagonistic to official policy goals

     18. Source of moral substitutes for national policy
     19. Source of functional alternatives to war
     20. Sanction for a national policy of isolationism

II. Domestic influences affecting foreign policy

  A. Relationships within the religious community
     21. Public opinion audience for a professional elite
     22. Source of motives for political action
     23. Moralizer of the appeals of war
     24. Moralizer of the tensions and guilt inherent in international conflict
     25. Source of intrapersonal conflict
     26. Consolation for the personal costs of conflict
     27. Source of group loyalties and activities compensating for feelings of inferior social status

  B. Relationships within the political community

     28. Sanction for secular pressure groups
     29. Sanction for party loyalties
     30. Determinant of voting behavior
     31. Source of ambiguous national loyalties
     32. Propaganda weapon in political controversy
     33. Source of instability in mass opinion
     34. Projection of non-rational values into the political arena
     35. Projection of dogmatic issues into the political arena
     36. Projection of secular issues into the political arena

  C. Relationships between religion and policy-makers

     37. Determinant of character-structure
     38. Criterion in selection and assignment
     39. Personal ministry to policy-makers
     40. Source of public support and prestige
     41. Pressure group directly influencing policy-makers
     42. Source of norms for the formulation of policy
     43. Source of norms for the criticism of policy
     44. Source of norms for personal conduct
     45. Source of norms for criticism of personal conduct
     46. Source of hostility to policy-makers
     47. Source of indifference to policy-makers
     48. Source of alienation from religion itself
     49. Distracting influence from the responsibilities of policy-makers
     50. Source of internal tensions for policy-makers
     51. Source of personnel

D. Relationships between religion and the nation-state
  52. Component of national character
  53. Component of national ideology
  54. Source of constitutional government and law
  55. Legitimization for state authority
  56. Sanction for the symbols of patriotism
  57. Rejection of state authority
  58. Source of symbols which conflict with state authority
  59. Source of norms for criticism of the structures and processes of policy-making within the government
  60. Sustainer of military morale

The Foreign Policy Apparatus (1962)

LIST OF ABBREVIATIONS

State Department Bureaus and Agencies

AID: Agency for International Development
INSPECTOR GENERAL, F.A.: Foreign Assistance
BUR. ECON. AFF.: Bureau of Economic Affairs
BUR. ED. & CULT. AFF.: Bureau of Educational and Cultural Affairs
BUR. I. O. AFF.: Bureau of International Organization Affairs
AM.: Bureau of Inter-American Affairs
E.: Bureau of European Affairs
AF.: Bureau of African Affairs
NE.: Bureau of Near Eastern and South Asian Affairs
FE.: Bureau of Far Eastern Affairs
BUR. INT. & RES.: Bureau of Intelligence and Research
BUR. ADMIN.: Bureau of Administration
BUR. SEC. & CON. AFF.: Bureau of Security and Consular Affairs
BUR. PUB. AFF.: Bureau of Public Affairs
CONG. REL.: Bureau of Congressional Relations

Executive Office of the President

S/A FOOD: Special Assistant to the President, Food for Peace
S/A NSC: Special Assistant, National Security Affairs
S/A CONG.: Special Assistant, Congressional Relations
CEA: Council of Economic Advisers
CIA: Central Intelligence Agency
NSC PL. BD.: National Security Council Planning Board
OEP: Office of Emergency Planning

AEC: Atomic Energy Commission
ACDA: Arms Control and Disarmament Agency
USIA: United States Information Agency
DIA: Defense Intelligence Agency

COMMERCE A/SEC.: Assistant Secretary for International Affairs
    TRAVEL SER.: United States Travel Service
LABOR A/SEC.: Assistant Secretary for International Affairs
H.E.W. DEP. A/SEC.: Deputy Assistant Secretary of Health, Education,
    and Welfare for International Affairs
P.O. INT. SERV. DIV.: International Service Division of Post Office
TREASURY INT. FIN.: Office of International Finance
AGRIC. FOREIGN AG. SERV.: Foreign Agricultural Service of the
    Department of Agriculture
JUSTICE I. & N.: Immigration and Naturalization Service
    FBI: Federal Bureau of Investigation
INTERIOR OFFICE OF TERR.: Office of Territories

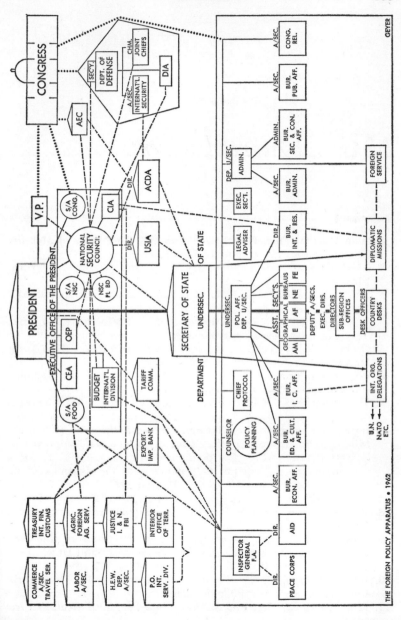

THE FOREIGN POLICY APPARATUS • 1962

GEYER

Notes and Acknowledgments

CHAPTER I

1. John Morton Blum, *Woodrow Wilson and the Politics of Morality* (Boston: Little, Brown and Company, 1956), p. 7.
2. Alexis de Tocqueville, *Democracy in America* (2 vols., New York: Vintage Books, 1956), I, p. 325.
3. Jerald C. Brauer, "The Rule of the Saints in American Politics," *Church History*, 27 (September, 1958), p. 240.
4. J. Milton Yinger, *Religion, Society, and the Individual* (New York: The Macmillan Company, 1957), p. 9.
5. Quoted in Louis Halle, *Civilization and Foreign Policy* (New York: Harper and Brothers, 1955), p. xvi.
6. Walter Lippmann, *U.S. Foreign Policy: Shield of the Republic* (Boston: Little, Brown and Company, 1943), p. 6.
7. This sharp criticism of theoretical models in the social sciences is developed more fully in Stanley H. Hoffmann, "International Relations: The Long Road to Theory," *World Politics*, XI (1959), pp. 346-377. The charge that the "structural-functional" approach of Talcott Parsons, which has dominated American sociology for a generation, has delayed an understanding of the dynamics of international conflict is made in Ralf Dahrendorf, "Toward a Theory of Social Conflict," *Conflict Resolution*, 2 (June, 1958), pp. 170-183.
8. Robert M. MacIver, *Conflict of Loyalties* (New York: Harper and Brothers, 1952), p. 1.
9. Ernst Troeltsch, *The Social Teaching of the Christian Churches*, trans. Olive Wyon (2 vols., London: George Allen and Unwin Ltd., 1931), II, pp. 1009-1013.
10. Herbert Butterfield, *Christianity, Diplomacy, and War* (New York: Abingdon-Cokesbury Press, n.d.), p. 68.
11. E. E. Schattschneider, *The Semisovereign People: A Realist's View*

of *Democracy in America* (New York: Holt, Rinehart and Winston, 1960), pp. 13, 67.

12. Frederick L. Schuman, *The Commonwealth of Man: An Inquiry into Power Politics and World Government* (New York: Alfred A. Knopf, 1952), p. 493.

13. Several of the most significant essays are to be found in Richard C. Snyder *et al.* (eds.), *Foreign Policy Decision-Making: An Approach to the Study of International Politics* (Glencoe, Illinois: The Free Press, 1962). Perhaps the most useful case study, from the standpoint of Christian ethics, is Robert C. Batchelder's history of the atom bomb, *The Irreversible Decision: 1939-1950* (Boston: Houghton-Mifflin Company, 1962).

14. Quoted by Hans Morgenthau, "Alone with Himself and History," *The New York Times Magazine* (November 13, 1960), p. 116.

15. Roger Hilsman, "The Foreign Policy Consensus: An Interim Research Report," *Conflict Resolution,* 3 (December, 1959), pp. 361-382.

16. See appendix for chart which depicts the complexity of the foreign policy apparatus—in simplified form!

17. George Kennan, *American Diplomacy, 1900-1950* (New York: The New American Library, 1952), p. 53.

18. Morgenthau has said that "the national interest" is a concept serving as "the main signpost that helps political realism to find its way through the landscape of international politics." See *Politics Among Nations: The Struggle for Power and Peace,* Third Edition (New York: Alfred A. Knopf, 1960), p. 5.

19. Charles O. Lerche, Jr., *Foreign Policy of the American People* (Englewood Cliffs, N. J.: Prentice-Hall, Inc., 1958), p. 12.

20. Gabriel Almond, *The American People and Foreign Policy* (New York: Harcourt, Brace and Company, 1950), pp. 140-141.

21. Will Durant, *The Story of Philosophy: The Lives and Opinions of the Greater Philosophers* (New York: Simon and Schuster, Inc., 1926), p. 1.

22. Robert Elder, *The Policy Machine: The Department of State and American Foreign Policy* (Syracuse University Press, 1960), p. 3.

CHAPTER II

1. Exodus 20:3, 5b. Except where otherwise noted, all biblical quotations are from the Revised Standard Version and are used by permission.

2. Psalm 101:1

3. Proverbs 20:28.

4. Norman H. Snaith, *The Distinctive Ideas of the Old Testament* (London: The Epworth Press, 1944), p. 49.

5. Acts 5:29.

6. Hebrews 13:17.

7. Paul Lehmann, "The Foundation and Pattern of Christian Behavior," in John A. Hutchison (ed.), *Christian Faith and Social Action* (New York: Charles Scribner's Sons, 1953), p. 110.

8. Salo Baron, *Modern Nationalism and Religion* (New York: Harper and Brothers, 1947), p. 253.

9. Herbert Butterfield, *op. cit.*, pp. 3-4.

10. Bernard Fensterwald, Jr., "The Anatomy of American Isolationism and Expansionism: Part I," *Conflict Resolution*, 2 (June, 1958), p. 136.

11. Robin M. Williams, Jr., "Religion, Value-Orientations, and Intergroup Conflict," *The Journal of Social Issues*, 12 (Spring, 1956), p. 19.

12. Robert S. Bilheimer, "Problems in Ecumenical Action," *Ecumenical Review*, 4 (July, 1952), p. 364.

13. *Ibid.*, p. 365.

14. *Ibid.*, pp. 360-363.

15. Robin M. Williams, Jr., *op. cit.*, p. 15.

16. Charles Y. Glock and Benjamin B. Ringer, "Church Policy and the Attitudes of Ministers and Parishioners on Social Issues," *American Sociological Review*, 21 (April, 1956), pp. 148-156.

17. Joseph H. Fichter, S. J., *Southern Parish* (Chicago: University of Chicago Press, 1951), chapter 20.

18. Samuel A. Stouffer, *Communism, Conformity, and Civil Liberties* (New York: Doubleday and Company, 1955), chapters 6 and 7.

19. G. Bromley Oxnam, *I Protest* (New York: Harper and Brothers Publishers, 1954).

CHAPTER III

1. Psalm 33:12.

2. Matthew 22:21.

3. Romans 13:1.

4. These observations are scattered throughout both volumes of James Bryce, *The American Commonwealth* (London: Macmillan and Company, 1889).

5. Leopold von Ranke, *Abhandlungen und Versuch* (Leipzig, 1872), p. 38. Quoted in Baron, *op. cit.*, p. 20.

6. Baron, *op. cit.*, p. 7.

7. Norman Hill and Doniver A. Lund, *If the Churches Want World Peace* (New York: The Macmillan Company, 1958), p. 90.

8. Denis W. Brogan, *Politics in America* (New York: Harper and Brothers, 1954), p. 174.

9. Reinhold Niebuhr, *The Irony of American History* (New York: Charles Scribner's Sons, 1952), p. 70.
10. Perry Miller, *The New England Mind: The Seventeenth Century* (New York: The Macmillan Company, 1939), p. 409.
11. John Cotton, "Limitation of Government," in Perry Miller (ed.), *The American Puritans: Their Prose and Poetry* (Garden City, New York: Doubleday and Company, Inc., 1956), pp. 85-86.
12. Miller, *The New England Mind, op. cit.,* pp. 418-419.
13. The colloquium, sponsored by the Fund for the Republic, was held in Washington in 1961. Miller's comment was published in the report, *The American Character: A Conversation* (Santa Barbara, Calif.: The Center for the Study of Democratic Institutions, 1962), p. 23.
14. Tocqueville, *op. cit.,* p. 142.
15. Reinhold Niebuhr, *Pious and Secular America* (New York: Charles Scribner's Sons, 1958), pp. 1-2.
16. Ralph Henry Gabriel, *The Course of American Democratic Thought: An Intellectual History Since 1815* (New York: Ronald Press, 1940), chapter 26.
17. Denis W. Brogan, *The American Character* (New York: Alfred A. Knopf, 1944), pp. 131-132.
18. Schuman, *op. cit.,* p. 118.
19. Joseph S. Roucek, *Social Control* (New York: D. VanNostrand Company, Inc., 1947), p. 186.
20. Walter Lippmann, *Essays in the Public Philosophy* (New York: The New American Library, 1956), p. 23.
21. Almond, *op. cit.,* pp. 59-60.
22. Thomas A. Bailey, *A Diplomatic History of the American People* (New York: Appleton-Century-Crofts, Inc., 1950), p. 187.
23. A. Mervyn Davies, *Foundation of American Freedom* (New York: Abingdon Press, 1955), p. 246.
24. Norman Hill, *International Relations: Documents and Readings* (New York: Oxford University Press, 1950), p. 482.
25. Niebuhr, *The Irony of American History, op. cit.,* p. 71.
26. Foster Rhea Dulles, *America's Rise to World Power: 1898-1954* (New York: Harper and Brothers, 1955), p. 85.
27. Don J. Hager, "Religious Conflict," *The Journal of Social Issues,* 12 (1956), p. 8.
28. Clinton Rossiter, *The American Presidency* (New York: The New American Library, 1956), pp. 74-75.
29. *Ibid.,* p. 12.
30. *Constitutional Government in the United States* (New York: Harper and Brothers Publishers, 1908), p. 68.

31. Charles W. Smith, *Public Opinion in a Democracy* (New York: Prentice-Hall, 1939), p. 196.

32. Blum, *op. cit.,* p. 85.

33. Norman Cousins, *Who Speaks for Man?* (New York: The Macmillan Company, 1953), pp. 252-253.

34. "The Christian Citizen in a Changing World," in *The Church and the International Disorder: An Ecumenical Study Prepared Under the Auspices of the World Council of Churches* (New York: Harper and Brothers Publishers, 1948), pp. 111, 113.

35. Quoted by John Robinson Beal, *John Foster Dulles: A Biography* (New York: Harper and Brothers Publishers, 1957), p. 131.

36. *Ibid.,* pp. 7-8.

37. *Ibid.,* pp. 138-152.

38. *Ibid.,* p. 13.

39. Richard Henry Tawney, *Religion and the Rise of Capitalism* (New York: Harcourt, Brace and Company, 1926), p. 175.

CHAPTER IV

1. Psalms 18:34, 39-40.

2. Matthew 10:34.

3. Matthew 24:6, 7.

4. Luke 7:8-9.

5. Luke 14:31.

6. Hugh C. Stuntz, *The United Nations Challenge to the Church* (New York: Abingdon-Cokesbury Press, 1948), pp. 72-73.

7. Arnold J. Toynbee, *A Study of History*. Abridgement of Volumes I-VI by D. C. Somervell (New York: Oxford University Press, 1951), p. 284.

8. Herbert Butterfield, *International Conflict in the Twentieth Century: A Christian View* (New York: Harper and Brothers, 1960), p. 18.

9. Butterfield, *Christianity, Diplomacy, and War, op. cit.,* p. 26.

10. Kennan, *American Diplomacy, 1900-1950, op. cit.,* pp. 98-99.

11. Raymond W. Mack and Richard C. Snyder, "The Analysis of Social Conflict: Toward an Overview and Synthesis," *Conflict Resolution,* 1 (June, 1957), pp. 216, 225.

12. The International Sociological Association, *The Nature of Conflict: Studies on the Sociological Aspects of International Tensions* (Paris: UNESCO, 1957), pp. 135-137.

13. Quoted in Paul A. Varg, *Missionaries, Chinese, and Diplomats* (Princeton: Princeton University Press, 1958), p. 82.

14. Thomas A. Bailey, *The Man in the Street: The Impact of American Public Opinion on Foreign Policy* (New York: The Macmillan Company, 1948), pp. 201-202.

15. Kennan, *American Diplomacy, op. cit.*, p. 42.
16. Hill and Lund, *op. cit.*, pp. 7-8. That Wilson's decision came only after profound internal tension is indicated below on p. 102.
17. William Warren Sweet, *The Story of Religion in America* (New York: Harper and Brothers, 1950), pp. 400-402.
18. Quoted in *ibid.*, pp. 402-403.
19. George Kennan, *Russia and the West under Lenin and Stalin* (Boston: Little, Brown and Company, 1961), p. 47.
20. Baron, *op. cit.*, p. 251.
21. Bailey, *The Man in the Street, op. cit.*, p. 188.
22. Harold Lasswell, "World Organization and Society," in Daniel Lerner and Harold Lasswell (eds.), *The Policy Sciences* (Stanford University Press, 1951), p. 111.
23. Batchelder, *op. cit.*, p. 213.
24. *Ibid.*, p. 210.
25. Charles Samuel Braden, *War, Communism, and World Religions* (New York: Harper and Brothers Publishers, 1953), p. 129.
26. "Let's Have a Showdown with Russia," *American Magazine*, 144 (August, 1947), p. 21.
27. Quoted by Beal, *op. cit.*, p. 313.
28. The policy of "containment" was first disclosed by Kennan in the heralded "Mr. X" article, "Sources of Soviet Conduct," *Foreign Affairs*, 25 (July, 1947), pp. 566-582.
29. Butterfield, *Christianity, Diplomacy, and War, op. cit.*, p. 104.
30. *Ibid.*, p. 43.
31. Samuel Lubell, *Revolt of the Moderates* (New York: Harper and Brothers, 1956), p. 82.
32. Wesley and Beverly Allinsmith, "Religious Affiliation and Politico-Economic Attitude: A Study of Eight Major U. S. Religious Groups," *Public Opinion Quarterly*, 12 (Fall, 1948), p. 386.
33. George Horsley Smith, "Liberalism and Level of Information," *Journal of Educational Psychology*, 39 (February, 1948), p. 65.
34. Lawrence H. Fuchs, *The Political Behavior of American Jews* (Glencoe, Illinois: The Free Press, 1956), p. 172.
35. Bailey, *A Diplomatic History, op. cit.*, p. 874.
36. Samuel Lubell, *The Future of American Politics* (Garden City, N. Y.: Doubleday and Company, 1956), p. 220.
37. George Gallup, "Protestants Voted GOP 62 Pct. to 38 in Election," *The Washington Post*, December 11, 1960, p. 11. Gallup's figures were disputed by IBM researchers who reported a 46 per cent Protestant support for Kennedy. See Theodore H. White, *The Making of the President 1960* (New York: Pocket Books, Inc., 1961), pp. 425-430.

38. Martin E. Marty, "Protestantism Enters Third Phase," *The Christian Century,* 78 (January 18, 1961), pp. 72-74.

39. Donald R. Matthews, *The Social Background of Political Decision-Makers* (Garden City, N. Y.: Doubleday and Company, 1954), p. 26.

40. Alan Geyer, *Comparative Studies in Religious and Political Affiliation in the 85th Congress* (Boston: Unpublished paper, March, 1957), pp. 2-5.

41. Ernest Best, "Facing Other Faiths," *The Christian Century,* 78 (January 11, 1961), p. 39.

CHAPTER V

1. Psalm 2:2-3.

2. Matthew 10:18.

3. Dietrich Bonhoeffer, *Ethics.* Edited by Eberhard Bethge and translated by Neville Horton Smith (New York: The Macmillan Company, 1955), p. 72.

4. Tocqueville, *op. cit.,* p. 317.

5. Thorsten V. Kalijarvi *et al., Modern World Politics,* Second Edition (New York: Thomas Y. Crowell Company, 1950), p. 37.

6. Varg, *op. cit.,* p. 56.

7. *Ibid.,* pp. 81-82.

8. Anson Phelps Stokes, *Church and State in the United States* (New York: Harper and Brothers, 1950), II, 429. Stokes says of Allen: "Some of his promotion plans and his relation to court intrigues were open to criticism, but his devotion to what he conceived to be the best interests of Korea was unquestioned."

9. William L. Neumann, "Determinism, Destiny, and Myth in the American Image of China," in George L. Anderson (ed.), *Issues and Conflicts: Studies in Twentieth Century American Diplomacy* (Lawrence, Kansas: University of Kansas, 1959), p. 19.

10. Bailey, *A Diplomatic History, op. cit.,* pp. 326-327.

11. Kenneth Scott Latourette, *The Chinese: Their History and Culture,* Third Edition Revised (New York: The Macmillan Company, 1946), pp. 389-394.

12. Varg, *op. cit.,* pp. 134-135.

13. Francis J. McConnell, *Public Opinion and Theology* (New York: The Abingdon Press, 1920), p. 24.

14. "Missions and Governments," Report of Commission VII (Edinburgh: World Missionary Conference, 1910), p. 95.

15. Chester Bowles, *Ambassador's Report* (New York: Harper and Brothers, 1954), p. 57.

16. See Clifford Manshardt (ed.), *The Mahatma and the Missionary* (Chicago: Henry Regnery Co., Inc., 1949).

17. Quoted in P. Oomman Philip, "Missions Under Fire in India," *The Christian Century*, 58 (August 15, 1956), pp. 944-945.

18. John A. DeNovo, "American Relations with the Middle East: Some Unfinished Business," in George L. Anderson (ed.), *Issues and Conflicts: Studies in Twentieth Century American Diplomacy* (University of Kansas Press, 1959), pp. 67-68.

19. James S. Coleman, "Social Cleavage and Religious Conflict," *The Journal of Social Issues*, 12 (1956), p. 52.

20. Lloyd M. Garrison, "The New Heart of Darkness," *The Reporter*, 23 (September 1, 1960), pp. 16-17.

21. Samuel Flagg Bemis, *The Latin American Policy of the United States* (New York: Harcourt, Brace and Company, 1943), pp. 390-391.

22. Quoted in Luke Ebersole, *Church Lobbying in the Nation's Capital* (New York: The Macmillan Company, 1951), p. 8.

23. Brogan, *The American Character, op. cit.*, p. 107.

24. Edmund A. Moore, *A Catholic Runs for President* (New York: The Ronald Press Company, 1956), pp. 16-17.

25. James H. Nichols, *Democracy and the Churches* (Philadelphia: The Westminster Press, 1951), pp. 358-359.

26. Lubell, *The Future of American Politics, op. cit.*, p. 238.

27. Nichols, *op. cit.*, pp. 261-262.

28. January 3, 1940. Quoted in Stokes, *Church and State in the United States*, II, p. 100.

29. Hugh A. Bone, *American Politics and the Party System* (2nd ed., New York: McGraw-Hill Book Company, 1955), pp. 182-183.

30. Hill and Lund, *If the Churches Want World Peace, op. cit.*, p. 54.

31. Varg, *op. cit.*, pp. 194-203.

32. John Leighton Stuart, *Fifty Years in China: The Memoirs of John Leighton Stuart, Missionary and Ambassador* (New York: Random House, 1954, p. 135.

33. Kenneth Scott Latourette, *A History of the Expansion of Christianity* (7 vols., New York: Harper and Brothers, 1945), VII, p. 149.

34. Varg, *op. cit.*, p. 263.

35. *Ibid.*, p. 272. See also J. W. Masland, "Missionary Influence upon American Far Eastern Policy," *Pacific Historical Review*, X (1941), pp. 279-296.

36. Kennan, *American Diplomacy, op. cit.*, p. 55.

37. Varg, *op. cit.*, p. 294.

38. Stuart, *Fifty Years in China, op. cit.*, p. xx. Acheson's Letter had concluded that "the ominous result of the civil war in China was beyond the control of the government of the United States. Nothing that this country did or could have done within the reasonable

limits of its capabilities could have changed that result; nothing that was left undone by this country contributed to it."

39. William Lee Miller, "A Theologically Biased View of Protestant Politics," *Religion in Life*, 21 (Winter, 1951-1952), p. 53.

40. Fensterwald, "The Anatomy of American 'Isolationism' and Expansionism," *op. cit.*, p. 121.

41. Almond, *The American People and Foreign Policy, op. cit.*, p. 239.

42. Charles Burton Marshall, *The Limits of Foreign Policy* (New York: Henry Holt and Company, 1954), p. 12.

43. Hill and Lund, *If the Churches Want World Peace, op. cit.*, p. 77.

44. Joseph P. Morray, *Pride of State: A Study in Patriotism and American National Morality* (Boston: Beacon Press, 1959), p. xv.

45. Yinger, *Religion, Society, and the Individual, op. cit.*, p. 238.

46. Hill and Lund, *If the Churches Want World Peace, op. cit.*, p. 45.

47. Lippmann, *U.S. Foreign Policy, op. cit.*, p. 7.

48. Marshall, *The Limits of Foreign Policy, op. cit.*, pp. 30-31.

49. John C. Bennett, *Christian Ethics and Social Policy* (New York: Charles Scribner's Sons, 1946), chapter II.

50. H. Jerry Voorhis, *The Christian in Politics* (New York: Association Press, 1951), pp. 26-27.

51. *Ibid.*, p. 96.

52. Warren B. Martin, "Weak Christian: Strong President," *The Christian Century*, 77 (August 17, 1960), pp. 946-947.

53. Accounts by Cobb and others which describe what Wilson himself called "the extraordinary isolation imposed upon the President" are reported in Morgenthau, "Alone with Himself and History," *op. cit.*, p. 25.

CHAPTER VI

1. Isaiah 11:9.

2. Psalm 91.

3. Romans 12:18-21.

4. John C. Bennett, *The Christian as Citizen* (New York: Association Press, 1955), p. 91.

5. Edmund Burke, *Reflections on the Revolution in France,* quoted in *The Oxford Dictionary of Quotations,* Second Edition (London: Oxford University Press, 1955), p. 102.

6. J. Milton Yinger, *Religion in the Struggle for Power: A Study in the Sociology of Religion* (Durham, North Carolina: Duke University Press, 1946), pp. 178-179.

7. *Ibid.*, pp. 187-189.

8. Kennan, *American Diplomacy, op. cit.*, p. 88.

9. Francis J. McConnell, *The Christian Ideal and Social Control* (Chicago: University of Chicago Press, 1932), p. 127.

10. Yinger, *Religion in the Struggle for Power, op. cit.,* p. 207.
11. Almond, *The American People and Foreign Policy, op. cit.,* pp. 170-171.
12. Foster Rhea Dulles, *America's Rise to World Power, op. cit.,* p. 120.
13. Hill and Lund, *If the Churches Want World Peace, op. cit.,* pp. 11-12.
14. Foster Rhea Dulles, *America's Rise to World Power, op. cit.,* p. 160.
15. *Ibid.,* p. 163.
16. Hill and Lund, *If the Churches Want World Peace, op. cit.,* p. 13.
17. *Ibid.,* p. 16.
18. Editorial, *The Christian Century,* 14 (October 20, 1937), p. 1287. Quoted in Foster Rhea Dulles, *America's Rise to World Power, op. cit.,* p. 180.
19. Foster Rhea Dulles, *America's Rise to World Power, op. cit.,* p. 180.
20. Tocqueville, *op. cit.,* I, p. 320.
21. Henry M. Wriston, *Diplomacy in a Democracy* (New York: Harper and Brothers, 1956), p. 106.
22. David Riesman, with Nathan Glazer and Reuel Denny, *The Lonely Crowd: A Study of the Changing American Character* (Abridged, Garden City, N. Y.: Doubleday and Company, Inc., 1956), p. 205.
23. William Lee Miller, *The Protestant and Politics* (Philadelphia: The Westminster Press, 1958), p. 19.
24. Murray B. Levin, *The Alienated Voter: Politics in Boston* (New York: Holt, Rinehart and Winston, Inc., 1960), p. 74.
25. Lawrence L. Durgin, "Honest Talk in Churches," *Social Action,* 23 (March, 1957), pp. 18-19.

CHAPTER VII

1. Isaiah 9:6-7.
2. Micah 4:1-3.
3. II Corinthians 5:17-20.
4. Bonhoeffer, *Ethics, op. cit.,* p. 77.
5. Erich Kahler, *Man the Measure: A New Approach to History* (New York: Pantheon Books, 1943), p. 6.
6. H. Richard Niebuhr, *Radical Monotheism and Western Culture* (New York: Harper and Brothers, 1960), pp. 33-34.
7. Quoted by Norman Bentwich, *The Religious Foundations of Internationalism* (London: George Allen and Unwin Ltd., 1933), p. 152.
8. George Kennan, *Realities of American Foreign Policy* (Princeton N. J.: Princeton University Press, 1954), pp. 18-19.
9. Hill and Lund, *If the Churches Want World Peace, op. cit.,* p. 10.
10. Stuntz, *op. cit.,* pp. 20-21.

11. Almond, *The American People and Foreign Policy, op. cit.*, p. 100.
12. Gove Hambidge, *The Story of FAO* (New York: D. Van Nostrand Company, Inc., 1955), pp. 89-93.
13. Ruth Rouse and Stephen Charles Neill (eds.), *A History of the Ecumenical Movement, 1517-1948* (Philadelphia: The Westminster Press, 1954), p. 709.
14. See the CCIA pamphlet, *Commission of the Churches on International Affairs*, pp. 5-6.
15. Personal interviews with O. Frederick Nolde and Richard M. Fagley.
16. Kenneth G. Grubb, "Christian Approach to International Affairs: A Criticism," *The Ecumenical Review*, 8 (July, 1956), p. 397.
17. Crane Brinton, *From Many, One: The Process of Political Integration—The Problem of World Government* (Cambridge: Harvard University Press, 1948), p. 112.
18. *These Rights and Freedoms* (New York: United Nations Department of Public Information, 1950), pp. 48-50.
19. Kenneth G. Grubb, "Christian Approach to International Affairs: A Criticism," *The Ecumenical Review*, 8 (July, 1956), p. 399.
20. *Evanston Speaks: Reports from the Second Assembly of the World Council of Churches* (New York: W.C.C., 1954), p. 47.
21. The ethical and political assumptions underlying "collective security" are discussed in A. F. K. Organski, *World Politics* (New York: Alfred A. Knopf, 1959), pp. 371-389.
22. Walter G. Muelder, *Foundations of the Responsible Society* (New York and Nashville: The Abingdon Press, 1959), p. 266.
23. Arnold J. Toynbee, "Spiritual Freedom is the Great Difference," *The New York Times Magazine*, January 15, 1961, p. 30.
24. Joseph M. Kitagawa, "Divided We Stand," *Religion in Life*, 27 (Summer, 1958), p. 343.
25. M. A. C. Warren, "Nationalism as an International Asset," *The International Review of Missions*, 44 (1955), pp. 387-390.
26. Walt Whitman Rostow, *The United States in the World Arena: An Essay in Recent History* (New York: Harper and Brothers, Publishers, 1960), p. 538.
27. Almond, *The American People and Foreign Policy, op. cit.*, p. 234.
28. Calvin J. Sutherlin, *American Seminaries and International Relations* (Berkeley, Calif.: The Pacific School of Religion, 1961, mimeographed).
29. "The Christian and His Vocation," Report of Section VI on the Laity, the Evanston Reports, *The Christian Century*, 71 (September 22, 1954), p. 1156.
30. Halle, *op. cit.*, p. 45.
31. Schuman, *op. cit.*, p. 106.

32. "Social Incubators," *The Washington Post,* October 28, 1962, p. E-6.
33. Harvey Seifert, "A Christian Reappraisal of Realism in Foreign Policy," *Religion in Life,* 29 (Winter, 1959-1960), p. 82.
34. Bertram Pickard, *Pacifist Diplomacy in Conflict Situations* (Philadelphia: Pacifist Research Bureau, 1943).
35. Colossians 1:19-20.

A Selected Bibliography

Almond, Gabriel: *The American People and Foreign Policy.* New York: Harcourt, Brace and Company, 1950.

Baron, Salo W.: *Modern Nationalism and Religion.* New York: Harper and Brothers, 1947.

Batchelder, Robert C.: *The Irreversible Decision: 1939-1950.* Boston: Houghton-Mifflin Company, 1962.

Beal, John Robinson: *John Foster Dulles: A Biography.* New York: Harper and Brothers, 1957.

Bennett, John C.: *Christian Ethics and Social Policy.* New York: Charles Scribner's Sons, 1946.

————: *Christians and the State.* New York: Charles Scribner's Sons, 1958.

———— (ed.): *Nuclear Weapons and the Conflict of Conscience.* New York: Charles Scribner's Sons, 1962.

Blum, John Morton: *Woodrow Wilson and the Politics of Morality.* Boston: Little, Brown and Company, 1956.

Bonhoeffer, Dietrich: *Ethics.* Edited by Eberhard Bethge and translated by Neville Horton Smith. New York: The Macmillan Company, 1955.

Butterfield, Herbert: *International Conflict in the Twentieth Century.* New York: Harper and Brothers, 1960.

Cullmann, Oscar: *The State in the New Testament.* New York: Charles Scribner's Sons, 1956.

Davies, A. Mervyn: *Foundation of American Freedom.* New York: Abingdon Press, 1955.

Dulles, Foster Rhea: *America's Rise to World Power: 1898-1954.* New York: Harper and Brothers, 1955.

Ebersole, Luke: *Church Lobbying in the Nation's Capital.* New York: The Macmillan Company, 1951.

Hill, Norman and Lund, Doniver A.: *If the Churches Want World Peace.* New York: The Macmillan Company, 1958.

Kennan, George: *American Diplomacy, 1900-1950.* New York: The New American Library, 1952.

Lefever, Ernest: *Ethics and United States Foreign Policy.* New York: Meridian Books, 1957.

Lippmann, Walter: *Essays in the Public Philosophy.* New York: The New American Library, 1956.

————: *U. S. Foreign Policy: Shield of the Republic.* Boston: Little, Brown and Company, 1943.

Mack, Raymond W. and Snyder, Richard C.: "The Analysis of Social Conflict: Toward an Overview and Synthesis." *Conflict Resolution,* 1 (June, 1957), pp. 212-48.

Miller, Perry: *The New England Mind: The Seventeenth Century.* New York: The Macmillan Company, 1939.

Miller, William Lee: *The Protestant and Politics.* Philadelphia: The Westminster Press, 1958.

Muelder, Walter G.: *Foundations of the Responsible Society.* Nashville: Abingdon Press, 1959.

Niebuhr, H. Richard: *Radical Monotheism and Western Culture.* New York: Harper and Brothers, 1960.

Niebuhr, Reinhold: *Christianity and Power Politics.* New York: Charles Scribners' Sons, 1940.

————: *The Irony of American History.* New York: Charles Scribners' Sons, 1952.

————: *Pious and Secular America.* New York: Charles Scribner's Sons, 1958.

Ramsey, Paul: *War and the Christian Conscience.* Durham: Duke University Press, 1961.

Rouse, Ruth and Neill, Stephen Charles (eds.): *A History of the Ecumenical Movement.* Philadelphia: The Westminster Press, 1954.

Schuman, Frederick L.: *The Commonwealth of Man: An Inquiry into Power Politics and World Government.* New York: Alfred A. Knopf, 1952.

Thompson, Kenneth W.: *Political Realism and the Crisis of World Politics.* Princeton University Press, 1960.

Troeltsch, Ernst: *The Social Teaching of the Christian Churches.* Translated by Olive Wyon. Two volumes. London: George Allen and Unwin Ltd., 1931.

Varg, Paul A.: *Missionaries, Chinese, and Diplomats: The American Protestant Missionary Movement in China, 1890-1952.* Princeton University Press, 1958.

Voorhis, H. Jerry: *The Christian in Politics.* New York: Association Press, 1951.

Yinger, J. Milton: *Religion, Society, and the Individual: An Introduction to the Sociology of Religion.* New York: The Macmillan Company, 1957.

Index of Names and Subjects